Dinner in a Basket

To my mother Shirley and my late father Alan:
your vegetable garden taught me that fresh, seasonal produce was always best.
Your garden has remained a great source of inspiration to me.

Also by the author:
Judith Cullen's Cooking Classes 2004

Dinner in a basket

Judith Cullen cooks from the market

Photography by Bill Nichol

Longacre Press

Acknowledgements

I'd like to extend a very special thank you to my friend Bill Nichol, the photographer (and my fellow stylist) for this book. We had such fun travelling to the various markets throughout New Zealand to photograph and sample what each had on offer. His professionalism, his 'good eye' and calm nature helped make every photo shoot not only a success but a pleasure.

I'd like to thank Barbara Larson and her team at Longacre Press for their support and enthusiasm for this project. A special thanks to designer, Christine Buess, for creating such a beautiful book and to Emma Neale for her clever editing.

I'm thankful to Penny Dawson of Pasta D'Oro for her professional culinary advice. And to Nick Wright from Ignition for his splendid cover design.

A big thank you to all the wonderful people at markets all over New Zealand who were so accommodating and enthusiastic about our 'Market Book'. Your passion and commitment to your produce is inspirational.

This book is copyright. Apart from any fair dealing for the purpose of private study, research, criticism or review, as permitted under the Copyright Act, no part may be reproduced by any process without prior permission of Longacre Press and the author.

The moral rights of Judith Cullen and Bill Nichol to be identified as the author and photographer of this work have been asserted.

© Text: Judith Cullen
© Photograph: Bill Nichol

Food styling by Judith Cullen and Bill Nichol

ISBN 978 1 877361 85 2

A catalogue record for this book is available from the National Library of New Zealand.

First published by Longacre Press, 2007
30 Moray Place, Dunedin, New Zealand.

Book design by Christine Buess
Cover design by Nick Wright
Printed by Printlink, Welliington

www.longacre.co.nz

Introduction 7

Cromwell Market
January 11

Nelson Market
February 25

The Marlborough Farmers' Market
March 41

Matakana Market
April 55

Auckland Markets
May 69

The Otago Farmers' Market
June and July 83

Wellington Markets
August and September 109

Hawkes Bay Markets
October and November 135

Otago Farmers' Christmas Market
December 161

Index 174

Introduction

Buying and eating the freshest seasonal produce makes enormous practical sense: it's time-saving, it supports local growers, it's a way to find the healthiest food – but it's also great fun. Shopping at markets is now fast becoming a preferred method of food shopping all over New Zealand.

For the customer, there is the wonderful opportunity to interact with growers and producers who are passionate and knowledgeable about their products, and who also, so often, clearly enjoy the privilege of selling in the buzzy, noisy atmosphere of a marketplace: so different from the ordinary supermarket environment. Market shopping encourages customers to put away their shopping list and just allow themselves to be tempted by all the seasonal offerings on display.

There's a real pleasure in being swept along by the continuous, lively traffic flow of a market – cars looking for parks, entertainers playing to the crowd, people walking with baskets, shopping bags, strollers and bikes, or pulling a variety of trolleys.

The morning markets are easy to identify and find. People of all ages use the market day as a social outing, often meeting friends for breakfast or brunch, and indulging in their favourite market treat along with the essential espresso. I've noticed many couples at markets, sharing the weekly food shop; and it's clear many people love to take advantage of the blending of cultures, tastes and ideas. Even children become familiar with the foods at the market, recognise their favourite stall, become more aware of where the food for the family meals comes from, and as a result, get more involved in the shopping. Vendors often thrive in the marketplace interaction too: enjoying conversations with the buyer, and valuing the encouragement and praise for their products.

Markets all over New Zealand are sited in a variety of places: some spaces are purpose-built with covered stalls facing a courtyard, with dining and socialising areas; others for practical reasons, are held in centrally convenient car parks. Yet many are located in stunning spots: from elegant railway stations to vineyards, and some are held in show grounds among beautiful mature trees.

Every weekend car parks and parks are transformed in the early hours of the morning with tents and tables. They become a kind of festive area that the vendors can fill with the very best produce that has been picked as recently as the night before, or even that morning.

Farmers' markets are a relatively new custom for New Zealand — and yet already each market reflects its own particular region. The seasonal aspect of many of the foods means that each individual market is also always changing. Whether you visit in summer, autumn, winter, or spring, and whether the market is weekly or held once a month, the market will bring new colours and tastes and be able to provide a wonderful regional selection. No matter which one you visit, you'll be spoilt for choice.

In this book I've built up a menu from a variety of regions and markets. I haven't included every market — new markets are opening up all the time. For this book I have travelled, with my photographer friend Bill Nichol, to a selection of markets throughout New Zealand. In the north we visited Matakana and Avondale, we travelled to Hawkes Bay, to Nelson and Blenheim, to the Wellington

markets, to glorious Central Otago and of course to the famous Otago Farmers' Market held at the Dunedin Railway Station. My main aim has been to think about the seasonality of our food choices, and to use the abundant selection of foods available to us all over New Zealand to provide healthy, interesting meals for friends and families.

I should also stress here that the recipes don't always rely on markets alone for the ingredients. Often purchases from other points of sale will be needed to complement the market fare.

For many people, going to the market is retail therapy. Gathering up your basket and heading to the nearest market can lift your spirits, give you a chance both to meet friends, and to evaluate the best buys. It also positively encourages you to get cooking, to ask some friends for dinner or prepare a lovely family meal.

If there is a farmers' market near you, get to know it, and become familiar with the produce on offer. I always take a tour around the market first so I know what's on every stall, so I can see where the best quality is, or the best value for money. Ask to taste products and talk to the vendor about their cooking and storing suggestions.

I love my own vegetable potager and wouldn't be without it. Being able to pick fresh herbs and lettuce leaves all year round, and plentiful zucchini or beans in the summer, gives me huge satisfaction. Yet for many people with no space for a garden, the market is there reliably, every week.

Markets are an all-year-round floor show; they put us back in touch with what's in season right now in our own regions.

Cromwell Market – January

Central Otago on a hot, dry summer's day is one of the best places to be in January. It has one of those very special climates where you know what to expect: it's guaranteed to be hot in the summer – and freezing cold in the winter.

Many Central Otago towns have changed hugely from their beginnings. Cromwell has a colourful history and has long been a stopover on the way to Queenstown and Wanaka.

I remember vividly our family journeys to Cromwell in the 1960s, our car towing a caravan as the train travelled beside us in the Cromwell Gorge, with only a little stone wall between us and the railway line. We would stop at the many roadside stalls selling ripe apricots, peaches and cherries – tempted by them even though we were anxious to get to Cromwell and leave the winding gorge behind.

Cromwell itself was approached over a wooden bridge which passed above the meeting of the green coloured water of the Clutha River and the blue water from the Kawarau; with its very narrow main street and its stone fronted shops it had real character. We often happily stopped for a walk around the museums or down to the old Chinese village by the water's edge.

Of course this all changed with the building of the Clyde Dam and the flooding of the lower part of the town. The new road bypassed the old town and Cromwell became a destination in its own right, rather

than somewhere you just passed through. Today this area is the location of the Cromwell Market – it's bordered by the water of Lake Cromwell and wrapped around the remaining old buildings of the former town; the character is still evident and the site exudes charm and personality. The river is now a lake, but it's still a beautiful area to explore, or to sit and picnic in.

The Cromwell market operates during the summer months, selling glorious produce and fruit from the most famous stone-fruit growing region of New Zealand. Cherries, apricots, nectarines, plums and peaches are plentiful – as in fact are blueberries and strawberries. There are also stalls that feature new season's garlic, herbs from the Culinary Herb Company, extra-virgin olive oil from Bannockburn, cheese from Blue River and Gibbston, and truffles from the Seriously Good Chocolate Company. These all add to the variety and diversity of a market where beautiful buckets of colourful flowers, organic lamb, beef and venison, fish, and even rabbits and pheasants are available. All of this, and you get spectacular views of Lake Dunstan and the Central Otago hills with every purchase! It's a unique, unforgettable setting.

Alongside this fabulous market site is Provisions, a store that sells ingenious jams, pickles and chutneys; and where they bake the best sticky buns – truly a necessity along with a coffee on any visit to the old town.

Given that we visited Cromwell in the middle of summer, I felt compelled to plan a menu that was suitable to barbecue and eat al fresco, so that we could take in the inspiring views of Central Otago.

In both the salmon fish cakes and the lamb kebab marinade, I've incorporated my favourite flavours: lemon grass, kaffir lime leaves and ginger (which are always available at the Mediterranean Markets in Wanaka and Queenstown). I've also used the amazing flavour of the local thyme honey.

The chicken jerk recipe is a traditional one from the Caribbean: it uses a lot of ground allspice and cinnamon, and the marinade gives the meat a blackened look, which works just as well on beef and lamb. I've suggested you serve this jerk with a fruity salad, which can include a selection of local stone fruit, and which I've topped off with a dressing that uses the glorious flavoured olive oil from Bannockburn.

It was difficult to choose which stone fruit to use for the dessert in this menu, but the winners were the peaches. However, both the amaretti stuffing and the semifreddo recipe could use plums, nectarines or apricots with equal success.

Surely everyone must want to have huge bowls of these colourful stone fruits on their kitchen benches at this time of the year, and to make the most of the sweet, sun-ripened fruit as snacks during the day or else in salads, cakes and desserts. Cromwell is the ideal spot to find them.

Whether you turn right to Wanaka or left to Queenstown it's worth stopping off here, and taking time to visit the ever growing population of vineyards and their fabulous restaurants – and of course a visit to the market should be essential on any vacation in Central Otago.

CROMWELL MARKET, CENTRAL OTAGO

Spicy Salmon Cakes

Pork and Lemon with Sweet Chilli Sauce

Chicken Jerk

Peach, Grapefruit and Pear Salad

Lamb Skewers with Lemon Grass and Ginger, served with Cucumber Pickle Salad

Peaches Stuffed with Amaretti Biscuits, served with Peach and Lemon Semifreddo

(each recipe serves 4–6 people)

Spicy Salmon Cakes

500 grams salmon or trout, skinned, boned and cubed
1 spring onion, thinly sliced
2 teaspoons fresh ginger, grated
½ cup fresh coriander, chopped
1 stalk fresh lemon grass, finely sliced
2 fresh kaffir lime leaves, diced finely

2 cloves garlic, crushed
1 tablespoon caster sugar
1 tablespoon fish sauce
100 grams green beans, thinly sliced
salt and pepper

sweet chilli sauce for dipping

In a bowl combine fish, spring onion, ginger, coriander, lemon grass, lime leaves, garlic, sugar and fish sauce.
Marinate for 30 minutes or so to let the flavours develop.
Transfer to a food processor and pulse to a coarse minced consistency.
Stir in the sliced beans, salt and pepper.
Using a dessert spoon, shape the fish mixture into balls, then flatten to a 1 cm cake using the palms of your hands.
Lightly oil a frying pan with olive oil. Add the fish cakes in batches and cook for 1 minute each side, or until golden and just cooked through.
Serve on a platter with sweet capsicum or sweet chilli sauce.

I buy plenty of fresh lemon grass and kaffir lime leaves when they're available at the market. Then I freeze them to have on hand.

Pork and Lemon *with Sweet Chilli Sauce*

4 lemons
olive oil
500 grams pork fillet
6 tablespoons sweet chilli sauce

Thinly slice the lemons and brush lightly with olive oil.
Slice the pork into thin rounds and brush with the sweet chilli sauce.
Place a lemon slice on top of each piece of pork and secure with a cocktail stick.
Cook over hot coals, in a frying pan or on a barbecue, lemon-side down first.
Cook for 1–2 minutes on each side until browned and cooked through.
Pile onto a serving platter and serve as finger food or with a green salad.

Chicken Jerk

½ cup ground allspice berries
½ cup brown sugar
6 cloves garlic, crushed
4 fresh chillies (red or green), de-seeded and chopped
2 bunches spring onions, sliced
1 teaspoon ground cinnamon
½ teaspoon ground nutmeg
salt and freshly ground black pepper, to taste
2 tablespoons soy sauce
1 kilo chicken legs or chicken thigh meat

Put everything except the chicken in a food processor and blend until smooth. (If refrigerated, the sauce will keep for 1–2 months.)

Rub the chicken with the jerk seasoning; be sure to rub underneath the skin and in the cavities.

Marinate 3–4 hours or overnight if possible.

Grill on a barbecue or bake at 200ºC (approx 15 minutes). Cooking over charcoal is best – the meat will have a smoked, pinkish look and the skin will be dark.

Serve with *Peach, Grapefruit and Pear Salad* (see following) and green salad leaves.

Jerk can also be used for pork – score the fat and rub all over the meat. It's also great for fish – use a firm-fleshed fish like groper or gurnard. Rub into the fish and grill or bake.

Peach, Grapefruit and Pear Salad

2 peaches, stoned and diced
2 grapefruit, peeled and divided into segments
1 small telegraph cucumber halved lengthways, de-seeded and sliced
1 nashi pear, cored and finely diced
1 crispy buttercrunch lettuce

Dressing
juice of 2 limes
¼ cup brown sugar
½ teaspoon salt
½ cup extra-virgin olive oil

Combine fruit and cucumber in a bowl.
Shake the dressing ingredients in a jar, pour over fruit and toss lightly.
Transfer to a serving dish lined with fresh, crisp salad leaves.

Lamb Skewers with Lemon Grass and Ginger
served with Cucumber Pickle Salad

1 kilo lamb back-straps or lamb fillets, diced into 2 cm pieces

Marinade
½ cup kecap manis
¼ cup peanut oil
1 red onion, chopped
2 sticks lemon grass, finely chopped
2 teaspoons ginger, grated
3 cloves garlic
1 small fresh chilli (red or green), de-seeded and chopped
1 tablespoon lemon juice

Place all marinade ingredients in a food processor, pulse to combine.
Place lamb in a ceramic bowl. Rub in the marinade and refrigerate for 1–2 hours.
Thread 4–5 pieces of lamb on each skewer. Barbecue or grill for 3–4 minutes on each side.
Serve with *Cucumber Pickle Salad* (see following).

Cucumber Pickle Salad

1 cup white vinegar
½ cup caster sugar
2 telegraph cucumbers, halved lengthways, de-seeded and sliced
1 fresh long green chilli, de-seeded and chopped
salt and freshly ground black pepper
½ cup coriander, chopped
½ cup unsalted roasted peanuts, chopped (optional)

In a saucepan heat the vinegar and sugar to dissolve the sugar. Cool.

Place the sliced cucumber in a bowl and add the cooled vinegar mixture and chilli. Season with salt and pepper and fold in coriander.

Refrigerate for 1 hour.

Place the lamb skewers on a serving platter. Spoon *Cucumber Pickle Salad* and chopped peanuts on top.

Peaches Stuffed with Amaretti Biscuits
served with Peach and Lemon Semifreddo

¾ cup coarsely crushed amaretti biscuits
¼ cup caster sugar
4 tablespoons cocoa powder
½ cup sweet white wine
2 tablespoons melted butter
6 medium-sized fresh free-stone peaches
   or nectarines

Put the crushed amaretti biscuits in a bowl with the caster sugar.
Add the cocoa powder through a sieve. Mix in 2 tablespoons of wine and the melted butter.
Cut each peach in half, remove the stone, and slice a small piece off the bottom to help the peaches sit flat.
Arrange cut side up in a shallow baking dish.
Pile a tablespoon of the amaretti mixture in the cavity of each peach. Pour over the remaining wine.
Bake 180ºC for 30 minutes or until the fruit is tender and golden on top.

Serve immediately with a slice of *Peach and Lemon Semifreddo* (see following).

Peach and Lemon Semifreddo

4 egg yolks
½ teaspoon vanilla essence
¾ cup caster sugar
4 tablespoons milk
zest of 1 lemon
⅓ cup lemon juice
2 cups cream
2 peaches, skinned, stoned and diced

Line a loaf tin or terrine dish with a double layer of tin foil.
Beat the egg yolks and vanilla with an electric beater until thick and creamy.
Combine the sugar, milk and lemon zest in a saucepan and heat gently, stirring until the sugar is dissolved.
Bring to the boil then add the lemon juice. Pour onto the egg yolks, whisking continuously. Cool.
Whip the cream. Fold into the egg mixture along with the diced peaches.
Pour the mixture into the lined mould. Freeze until firm – 24 hours is best.
Serve with the *Stuffed Peaches* (above).

Nelson Market – February

I remember going to this market many years ago, when our children were very young, and buying the aeroplanes made out of beer cans, and the balloon animals. We might not be looking for that kind of treat any more, but we still go for the food. For the 25 plus years that this market has been running on the same site, it has always had excellent food stalls, selling real bread, German sausages, cheeses, and the freshest fruits and vegetables – nurtured to maturity and sold less than 24 hours after being picked.

The Nelson region has always had a strong reputation for fresh produce, and well before the current surge in farmers' markets, the farming district hosted many, many roadside stalls which sold everything from delicious berries to cheap tomatoes and freshly cut lettuces. All those New Zealanders who migrated to the Tahunanui camping ground during the summer school holidays will know what I mean.

Today much of the former farming area is now housing, but the Nelson Market has the same great food stalls. It draws large crowds every Saturday morning and provides not only food for the week, but also an eclectic range of artists' work from around the Nelson region.

The food stalls are dotted around a transformed car park, and on a leisurely walk you can buy an amazing selection of very reasonably priced goods.

Many stands provide cooked products – a rather nice aspect of visiting all

these early morning markets is that you don't have to eat breakfast at home. They all have wonderful hot food: from waffles and pancakes to sausages and other cooked breakfasts. For me, on an early morning visit, the fresh espresso stall is always a vital necessity – and of course this is where you can then buy your freshly roasted coffee for the week. (If you get used to the taste of freshly ground coffee, you soon learn how nasty prepackaged ground coffee is!)

Every time I visit a market I get carried away with the selection – Bill was always very useful on our market excursions, helping me to the car with my overloaded basket – but I have to confess I was particularly busy in Nelson. I came home with two baskets full and even bought a chilly bin to help get food back to Dunedin safely.

What did I have? Bread, cheese, smoked seafood, German meat products, a huge array of organic fruit and vegetables (if Puglia is called the fruit bowl of Italy, then I think the Nelson/Marlborough region would be a close runner-up for that title in New Zealand), and fresh corn. (In fact at the corn stall, I bought a large paper bag of what I thought was corn, but when I arrived home I found it was potatoes – however they were delicious.) I also bought the biggest bunches of fresh basil I have ever seen and … berries of all types, apples, nashi pears, olive oil and red onions – I have always associated Nelson with these gorgeous red beauties.

Listening to the stall holders chatting with customers is always interesting. They discuss all sorts of things – including the quantity of sunshine hours, the rain or lack of it, and how the weather has affected their crops. The weather is important for these passionate food producers, who are hell-bent on delivering their best produce to the market each week.

The market at Nelson provided me with a large assortment of ingredients and beautiful flavours. The bright colours of the ingredients matched my Christine Boswijk's vividly coloured platters.

From the intense green of the soup to the deep purple of the blueberry and sour cream cake, the ingredients of each recipe seemed to have their own lively visual appeal.

NELSON MARKET

Green Garden Soup

Smoked Fish Roulade with Lemon and Caper Sauce

Pork Fillet Stuffed with Spinach and Plums, served with Sweet Plum Sauce

Aubergine, Tomato and Gruyère Torte

Roasted Beetroot with Red Onions and Chorizo, topped with Feta and Pine Nuts

Blueberry Sour Cream Cake

(each recipe serves 4–6 people)

Green Garden Soup

2 tablespoons olive oil
2 leeks, sliced
1 red onion, diced
4 celery stalks, sliced
2 cloves garlic, crushed
1 potato, peeled and chopped
2 zucchini, chopped
1 bunch spinach leaves, stalks removed
¼ cup lemon juice
2 litres chicken or vegetable stock
1 cup peas, fresh or frozen
2 cups shredded lettuce
¼ cup parsley, chopped
2 tablespoons mint leaves
salt and freshly ground black pepper

In a large saucepan sauté the leeks, red onion, celery and garlic in the olive oil.
Add the potato, zucchini, spinach and lemon juice.
Pour in the stock and simmer gently for 15–20 minutes.
Add the peas and lettuce and cook for a further 5 minutes.
Stir through the parsley and mint.
Process in batches in a food processor or use a stick blender until smooth and silky.
Re-heat and season with salt and freshly ground black pepper.
Serve hot or chilled.
To serve: if the soup is too thick, add more stock before re-heating and serving.

Chicken or vegetable stock can be replaced with fish stock. To serve: mound cooked fish strips in centre of each plate and ladle over soup. Serve at once.

Smoked Fish Roulade
with Lemon and Caper Sauce

250 grams smoked fish
5 eggs, separated
5 tablespoons cream
zest of 1 lemon
2 tablespoons lemon juice

3 tablespoons pecorino cheese, grated
salt and freshly ground black pepper
3 hard-boiled eggs, chopped
2 tablespoons parsley, chopped
4 tablespoons Parmesan cheese, grated (optional)

In food processor blend smoked fish, egg yolks and cream.
Transfer to a bowl, add the lemon zest, lemon juice, grated pecorino cheese and salt and pepper.
Whisk egg whites to firm peaks and fold in the fish mixture.
Spread into a lined Swiss roll tin, and bake at 200ºC for 10–15 minutes.
When firm to touch, turn out onto a clean tea towel and spread with the *Lemon and Caper Sauce* (see following). Add a row of chopped hard-boiled eggs.
Roll up like a Swiss roll.
Slide onto a plate and garnish with parsley and grated Parmesan cheese (optional).

Lemon and Caper Sauce

50 grams butter
2 tablespoons flour
1 cup milk
3 tablespoons parsley, chopped

2 tablespoons capers
zest of 1 lemon
2 tablespoons lemon juice
salt and freshly ground black pepper

In a saucepan melt the butter, add flour and cook until bubbly to make a roux.
Pour in the milk, all at once, stir until thick.
Add parsley, capers, lemon zest and juice.
Season with salt and freshly ground black pepper.

Pork Fillet Stuffed with Spinach and Plums
served with Sweet Plum Sauce

500 grams pork fillets (approx 2 fillets)
1 bunch spinach, trimmed and washed
6 plums, stoned
1 tablespoon extra-virgin olive oil
pinch cinnamon
juice of 1 lemon
salt and freshly ground black pepper
l packet Cured Blackforest Ham
   (from the Bratwurst Grill*)*

Sweat the plums in olive oil in a small saucepan on low heat until soft. Drain.
Blanch the spinach in boiling water until limp. Squeeze out excess liquid.
Combine spinach, cinnamon, lemon juice, and salt and pepper.
Split pork fillets through the middle, but not all the way through. Open out each fillet like a book.
Layer with spinach leaves and plum halves.
Fold the pork fillet edges together – being careful to keep the filling inside.
Wrap each fillet with slices of Cured Blackforest Ham. Tie string around each to hold in place.
Place the wrapped pork fillets in a baking dish. Drizzle with olive oil.
Bake at 180ºC for 30–40 minutes.
Serve with *Sweet Plum Sauce* (see following).

Sweet Plum Sauce

500 ml water
2 cups caster sugar
½ cup red wine
1 stick cinnamon
2 whole cloves
1 whole mace
1 kilo plums, halved and stoned

Put all the ingredients except the plums into a large saucepan and bring to the boil for 20 minutes.
Add the plums to the syrup and cook for 30 minutes or until the plums have become mushy and lost their shape.
Purée in a food processor or press the mixture through a sieve.
The sauce can be used immediately or refrigerated and re-heated.

Aubergine, Tomato and Gruyère Torte

Tomato Sauce

2 tablespoons olive oil
1 onion, finely chopped
1 kilo ripe tomatoes, skinned and diced
1 tablespoon tomato paste
¼ cup parsley, chopped
¼ cup basil leaves, chopped
½ teaspoon salt
freshly ground black pepper

Torte

2 medium-sized aubergines, sliced
olive oil
5 eggs
¼ cup pecorino cheese, grated
2 cups Gruyère cheese, grated

In a saucepan, sauté the onion in olive oil until soft.
Add the tomato paste and tomatoes, simmer until the tomatoes are soft and the mixture has reduced and thickened.
Add the chopped herbs and seasoning.

Brush the aubergine slices with olive oil. Grill or barbecue each side until golden.

In a small bowl whisk the eggs. Stir in the grated pecorino cheese.
Line a loaf tin or terrine dish with tin foil.
Place a layer of aubergine slices on the base and along the sides of dish.
Cover the base with ⅓ of the tomato sauce, topped with ⅓ of the Gruyère cheese, ⅓ of the egg mixture and a layer of aubergine slices.
Repeat the layers twice more, finishing with a layer of aubergine.
Bake at 180ºC for 50 minutes or until set.
Stand for 20–30 minutes before removing from dish. Slice and serve.

Roasted Beetroot with Red Onions and Chorizo, topped with Feta and Pine Nuts

4–5 medium-sized beetroot, peeled and diced in 2 cm pieces
2 red onions, peeled, halved and sliced lengthways
3–4 tablespoons olive oil
1 tablespoon balsamic vinegar
2 chorizo sausages, sliced thinly
¾ cup pine nuts, lightly roasted
200 grams feta cheese, diced
1 cup rocket leaves
2–3 tablespoons Nelson Extra-Virgin Olive Oil
sea salt crystals and freshly ground black pepper

In a large baking dish toss the beetroot and red onion slices in the olive oil
and balsamic vinegar.
Bake at 200ºC for 30 minutes or until cooked.
Sauté the sliced chorizo in a frying pan until it starts to crisp.
Toss chorizo through the cooked beetroot and onions.
Transfer the beetroot mixture to a serving platter, sprinkle with
the cubed feta cheese and pine nuts.
Toss the rocket leaves in extra-virgin olive oil and pile on top of the beetroot salad.
Sprinkle with sea salt and freshly ground black pepper before serving.

Blueberry Sour Cream Cake

1 cup caster sugar
250 grams butter
2 eggs
2 cups flour
1 tablespoon baking powder
1 vanilla pod, halved and seeded

2 cups blueberries, fresh or frozen
2 cups sour cream
½ cup caster sugar
½ teaspoon vanilla essence
3 egg yolks
2 tablespoons redcurrant jelly

In a bowl cream the butter and sugar.
Beat in the eggs one at a time.
Fold in the flour, baking powder and vanilla seeds.
Spread the batter into the bottom of a greased 26 cm spring-form cake tin.
Pile the blueberries on top.
Beat together sour cream, sugar, vanilla, and egg yolks. Pour over the blueberries.
Bake for 55–60 minutes at 160ºC or until set.
Brush with melted redcurrant jelly to glaze.

Note: this cake takes some time to set in the middle. I often make it in a shallower baking dish which will take less time.

The Marlborough Farmers' Market – Blenheim – March

Thankfully, the Marlborough Farmers' Market in Blenheim is held on a Sunday morning – so Bill and I could still make it after an early drive from Nelson. It was a fabulous day, perhaps made more so by the fact that starting out so early meant we drove through fog until we emerged onto the sunny Blenheim plain.

The AMP show ground is a short car trip from the outskirts of Blenheim and provides the perfect site: if it rains, stall holders can move to the covered sheep yards. Yet Blenheim certainly does summer well: it's surrounded by dry golden hills, and endless rows of vines that provide juice for wineries to make into gorgeous wines.

This market is the epitome of farmers' markets. The stalls are shaped to attract buyers and yet still have open spaces for people to sit and enjoy the live music. The market had a picnic feel and a relaxed atmosphere: adults and children were happy and slowly wandered from one stall to another. People of all ages were buying their produce for the week, knowing the beans were probably picked that morning or the night before and that the courgettes would still be crisp.

The market has everything from lamb (a special breed called Dorper, raised beside the salt-producing Lake Grassmere), salmon, wild venison sausages, two bread stalls, olive oil, hazelnuts, saffron, honey, jams, chutneys, and fruit – including fresh figs and a stall selling five or six varieties of plums. The vendor at the plum stall was so passionate about her plums that she sliced wedges off each

variety for customers to taste, and could fill you in with everything you needed to know about her plums. Fabulous stuff!

The fresh corn stall was amazingly attractive. The produce was presented complete with corn stems and the cobs still attached. Tomatoes too were eye-catching: their appearance ranged from large and deep red, to small, teardrop-shaped, and yellow.

I bought cos lettuce and celeriac plants for my garden from a stall with a huge selection of vegetable and herb plants on offer. Lettuce or fresh coriander takes little space in any garden and being able to cut your own can give you a huge amount of satisfaction.

At this time of the year the cut flowers are stunning – we saw buckets of calla lilies, gentians, sunflowers and brightly coloured gerberas. I always think you need to buy at least three bunches to fill a large vase: they'll look stunning in your kitchen and will continue to give a sense of life and vibrancy to your busy week.

I met up with a friend, Ros, who once travelled with me in one of my tour groups to Sicily, where we visited huge and famous markets like the Vucciria in Palermo. The Blenheim Market was a perfect meeting place: giving us the opportunity to chat and make comparisons as we walked around the displays. She was very keen to show off this dynamic market and to illustrate how it provides essential and excellent produce for the local community. And for visitors, too: it was inspiring shopping here – Bill can confirm my basket was overflowing and heavy once again.

The selection of fruit and vegetables available at this time of the year, and the appeal of the Blenheim Market, made shopping and selecting a menu such fun.

The impressive corn can be used for so many recipes: soups, salads, salsas or as a vegetable in its own right. Corn chowder is always delicious and is still a welcome choice even when the season's temperatures are quite warm. It can be combined with a variety of seasonal vegetables, and capsicums and zucchini were also in abundance here.

Colourful capsicums and tomatoes combined with basil top the delicious rice pancakes. In fact anything could be used to top these versatile pancakes: from sautéed mushrooms and bacon to a selection of seafood – especially seafood from Marlborough and the Sounds.

For this menu, I bought a leg of the Dorper lamb I've already mentioned, boned and butterflied it, then rubbed it with fennel seeds and orange. This is an easy, tasty method of cooking a leg of lamb, and although here it is accompanied with a simple potato dish and a green bean salad with rocket and pumpkin, it is equally delicious sliced warm and served with some of the great bread sold at the Blenheim Market and topped with a homemade chutney or pesto.

I used fresh hazelnuts from the market to create a wonderful flavour in the dessert with fresh pears. This cake keeps well because of the addition of sour cream. It remains moist for days – if you can keep it for that long.

I have always made quince paste each year from the enormous amount of quinces I get from the espaliered trees against our house. However, recently I have also been making plum paste. The fantastic plum stall at this market gave me a chance to buy more plums and make more paste, which I use throughout the year on antipasto and cheese platters. It's easy to make and will reward you with an intense, rich flavour.

THE MARLBOROUGH FARMERS' MARKET, BLENHEIM

Leek and Corn Chowder

Risotto Pancakes with Tomato and Grilled Capsicum

Potatoes with Rosemary, Cherry Tomatoes and Black Olives

Butterflied Leg of Lamb rubbed with Orange and Fennel Marinade, served with Red Capsicum and Mustardseed Marmalade

Green Beans, Caramelised Pumpkin and Roasted Walnut Salad

Pear and Hazelnut Crumble Cake

Cheeses with Plum Paste and Crackers

(each recipe serves 4–6 people)

Leek and Corn Chowder

2 tablespoons olive oil
3 medium leeks
6 bacon rashers
1 medium kumara
1 medium potato
2 medium carrots
2 zucchini
3 cups chicken stock
3 cobs of fresh corn, husks removed
2 tablespoons butter
2 tablespoons flour
1 cup milk
handful of chopped parsley

Dice leeks, bacon, kumara, potato, carrots and zucchini into 1 cm cubes.

In a large saucepan, sauté the leeks and bacon in the olive oil until cooked.

Stir in the kumara, potato and carrots. Pour the chicken stock over the mixture. Cover and bring to the boil.

Reduce the heat and simmer for 15 minutes or until vegetables are just tender.

Add the corn and zucchini and simmer for a further 5 minutes.

In a small saucepan melt the butter. Add the flour and cook for 1 minute, stirring constantly to make a roux.

Pour in the milk and stir until mixture boils and thickens.

Slowly stir the sauce into the vegetable and corn mixture.

Bring back to the boil, add chopped parsley and season with salt and freshly ground black pepper before serving.

Risotto Pancakes with
Tomato and Grilled Capsicum

2 tablespoons olive oil
2 large shallots, finely chopped
1 clove garlic, crushed
1 teaspoon fresh thyme, chopped
½ cup Arborio rice
¼ cup dry white wine
2 cups vegetable or chicken stock, hot

½ cup freshly grated Parmesan cheese
½ cup fresh breadcrumbs
salt and freshly ground black pepper

2 eggs, lightly beaten

Risotto

In a saucepan heat the olive oil. Sauté the shallots, garlic and thyme until soft.
Stir in the rice and pan-fry for 1 minute. Add the wine and cook until liquid has been absorbed.
Pour in the hot stock, a ladleful at a time, stirring constantly. Keep adding the stock as the previous ladleful is absorbed. Cook for 20–25 minutes over a low heat, until all the stock is absorbed and the rice is soft.
Add grated Parmesan cheese, breadcrumbs and seasonings. Cover and cool.

To make Pancakes

Stir the eggs into cooled rice mixture.
Put a large spoonful of the rice mixture into a small, oiled, heated frying pan. Spread mixture out to make a flattish pancake.
Fry until golden, then carefully turn and fry the other side for a further 1–2 minutes.
Repeat to make 6 pancakes.

(recipe cont'd next page)

Tomato and Grilled Capsicum

1 tablespoon olive oil
2 red capsicums, halved, de-seeded and grilled until blackened
6 ripe tomatoes, quartered
1 tablespoon caster sugar
2 tablespoons balsamic vinegar
1 teaspoon Worcester sauce
1 teaspoon lemon juice
sea salt and freshly ground black pepper
fresh basil or chopped parsley (garnish)

Cover blackened capsicums with a tea towel, allow to cool. Peel off skin and slice.

Heat the oil in a frying pan, add the tomatoes. Sauté on a high heat for a minute or so, then add capsicum slices.

Reduce the heat, and add the sugar, balsamic vinegar, Worcester sauce and lemon juice.

Cook gently for 2–3 minutes. Check the seasoning.

To serve: top the pancakes with the caramelised tomatoes and capsicums. Garnish with fresh basil or chopped parsley.

Potatoes with Rosemary, Cherry Tomatoes and Black Olives

1 kilo potatoes – Agria or good baking potatoes
3–4 tablespoons olive oil
4 tablespoons fresh rosemary, chopped
1 small bulb garlic, cloves peeled but left whole
flaky sea salt and freshly ground black pepper
20 cherry tomatoes
20 black olives
handful of fresh parsley, chopped

Peel the potatoes and dice into 1 cm cubes. Par-boil in salted water for 10 minutes. Drain and blot with kitchen paper to absorb excess moisture.
In a large frying pan heat the oil. Add the par-cooked potatoes, rosemary, garlic, a little salt and lots of freshly ground black pepper.
Leave to brown on a medium heat, tossing occasionally.
After 10 or so minutes – when the potatoes are golden, crispy and crunchy – add the tomatoes and olives. Mix in gently.
Cook for a few minutes until the tomatoes are warm and start to go limp.
Sprinkle the dish with chopped parsley and serve immediately.

Butterflied Leg of Lamb *rubbed with Orange and Fennel Marinade, served with Red Capsicum and Mustardseed Marmalade*

*2.25 kilo leg of lamb, boned and butterflied
 (try Dorper lamb)
2 teaspoons fennel seeds, dry roasted
2 cloves garlic, crushed
2 teaspoons orange zest
juice of 1 orange
¼ cup lemon-infused olive oil
¼ cup fresh oregano, chopped*

In a mortar and pestle grind the fennel seeds roughly and combine with the crushed garlic, orange zest and juice, lemon-infused olive oil and oregano.

Trim the excess fat from the lamb. Open out flat, skin side down.

Rub the marinade over the lamb to cover the surface.

Cover and refrigerate for 2 hours or overnight.

Place lamb in a roasting dish.

Roast at 200ºC for 30 minutes. Turn over and cook for a further 15–20 minutes until browned. Alternatively cook in a covered barbecue.

Rest the lamb in warm place for at least 10 minutes before slicing.

Serve with *Red Capsicum and Mustardseed Marmalade* (see following).

Red Capsicum and Mustardseed Marmalade

- 2 large red capsicums, de-seeded and thinly sliced, lengthways
- 2 teaspoons olive oil
- 2 fresh bay leaves
- 2 cups white sugar
- ¼ cup sultanas
- 1 tablespoon black mustard seeds
- ½ cup dry red wine
- ½ cup white wine vinegar

Heat oil in a saucepan and sauté capsicum with the bay leaves over a medium heat until capsicum is tender.
Add sugar and stir over low heat until sugar dissolves.
Add sultanas, mustard seeds, red wine, white wine vinegar and ½ cup water.
Cook over medium heat until reduced to a syrupy consistency.
Serve with *Butterflied Leg of Lamb* or store in clean dry jars for 6–12 months.

Green Beans, Caramelised Pumpkin and Roasted Walnut Salad

500 grams green beans, trimmed
½ medium butternut pumpkin, peeled and diced
2 cups walnut halves (optional – tossed in 1 tablespoon olive oil and 1 teaspoon cajun spice mix)
2 tablespoons extra-virgin olive oil
4 tablespoons maple syrup
1 tablespoon balsamic vinegar
flaky sea salt and freshly ground black pepper
2 cups of mesclun salad mix or rocket leaves
2 tablespoons extra-virgin olive oil for dressing
1 tablespoon balsamic vinegar for dressing
handful of Parmesan cheese, shaved with a potato peeler

Place pumpkin in a large baking dish.
Mix the olive oil, maple syrup, and balsamic vinegar together and pour over the pumpkin and toss.
Bake at 200ºC for 15 minutes.
Remove from the oven, add the beans to the pumpkin and toss.
Return to the oven and bake for a further 10 minutes.
Bake the walnuts in a small baking dish until they start to look golden.
When tender, transfer the vegetables to a serving platter, sprinkle the walnuts on top, season with salt and pepper.
Toss mesclun salad or fresh rocket leaves, and shaved Parmesan cheese, in extra-virgin olive oil and balsamic vinegar.
Pile salad leaves on top of the bean and pumpkin mixture and serve.

Pear and Hazelnut Crumble Cake

250 grams butter
1 cup caster sugar
2 eggs
1 teaspoon vanilla
2 cups flour
1 teaspoon baking soda
1 teaspoon baking powder
1 cup sour cream

3 pears, peeled, cored, quartered and sliced into 3

Crumble
¼ cup brown sugar
¼ cup caster sugar
½ cup chopped toasted hazelnuts, skinned
(combine all ingredients)

In a bowl cream the butter and sugar until light and fluffy.
Add the eggs, one at a time, and beat after each addition.
Add the remaining cake ingredients and combine gently with a metal spoon or silicone scraper.
Spoon the batter into a greased 26 cm spring-form cake tin.
Place the sliced pears, cut side down, in a circle on top of the batter.
Sprinkle the crumble mixture evenly over the top.
Bake at 180ºC for 60 minutes, or until firm to the touch.
Dust with icing sugar just before serving.

Plum Paste

2 kilos dark, red-fleshed plums, halved and stoned
2 tablespoons lemon juice
2 ½ cups caster sugar

Combine plums, lemon juice and 1 cup water in a large saucepan. Bring to the boil.
Simmer for 15 minutes until the plums are soft. Strain, discarding the liquid.
Process the plums in a food processor until smooth.
Transfer the purée to a clean saucepan.
Add the sugar and simmer, stirring frequently (approx 45–50 minutes).
Once the mixture begins to thicken, stir constantly to prevent sticking.
Cook until the paste is very thick – when you pull a spatula through the plum mixture it will form a trail.
Transfer the paste to a ceramic dish.
Cool to room temperature. Cover and refrigerate until firm.
Keep in an airtight container – it will keep for up to 6 months.
Serve with local cheeses and crackers.

Matakana Market
North Auckland – April

Bill and I visited Matakana in autumn. It is a purpose-built village market which offers a unique, friendly atmosphere for shoppers away from the goings-on in the big city close by. The produce is beautifully presented under the wooden eaves in cane baskets piled high to showcase their very best quality: from the stacked, wholesome looking bread with its wonderful aroma, to the vibrant bottles of olive oil, and the many preserves on offer.

Matakana has a lively ambience. People continually stream into the market surrounds and are immediately tempted by the coffee, breakfast and brunch options – which on the day we visited included whitebait fritters, waffles and freshly cooked wontons.

The stalls are not large so the whole area has a sense of friendliness and intimacy. Stall holders enjoy talking to shoppers and are keen to show their passion and dedication for growing and selling their produce. Boutique fruit and vegetable gardeners sell small quantities of exquisite produce – and shoppers were obviously excited about finding such treasures. A highlight for me was the stall which had the most gorgeous red chillies that looked like wax flowers, and tiny little aubergines hanging from branches, like miniature grapes.

The visual appeal of stalls like these, with their striking colours, the artful arrangement of goods, and sometimes the sheer attraction of seeing healthy produce en masse, is where markets have it over all other types of shopping.

These features – as well as the fact that a market changes each week, so you need to wander round for an initial 'scout' to see what's what – really encourage those spontaneous purchases that lead you to new discoveries. Then you can go home and have fun planning a recipe and meal around them.

I left Matakana with a basket full of typical autumn goodies, which led to this menu: a fabulous yet simple pie using silverbeet, apples and pine nuts. I also included market-bought blue cheese, and topped the pie with a stir fry of tomatoes, the little aubergines, chillies and fresh coriander.

As I was leaving the market I stopped at the fresh tuna stall. I ended up going home with a variety of tuna: dinner at my brother's house that night consisted of a 'tuna tasting', served with a salsa of feijoas, avocado and persimmon, with lime juice and fresh coriander. Tuna is a healthy food choice and must be cooked so it's rare in the middle. It's quick, and couldn't be simpler, especially now that's it readily available freshly caught. I also served the fish with a tasty selection of red vegetables flavoured with crispy Florence fennel. (This is not to be confused with the herbaceous variety. It grows like carrots and can be planted in the spring and autumn – it has a slightly aniseedy flavour – and I hope we'll start to see more of it on sale around the country.)

The North Island has an abundance of feijoas and persimmons at this time of the year – both are delicious eaten raw. Persimmons can also be used in their soft state – like old bananas – for baking. The little cakes in this menu are perfect for this, and the passionfruit made an equally perfect flavour for the icing.

MATAKANA MARKET, NORTH AUCKLAND

Seafood Filo Pies with Capsicum Sauce

Silverbeet, Apple and Parmesan Pie,
served with Aubergine and Tomato Sauce

Fresh Tuna with Avocado and
Diced Tomato Guacamole

Grilled Tomatoes with Braised Red Onion,
Red Capsicum and Florence Fennel

Sweet Potato and Sage Ricotta Tart

Persimmon Cakes with Passionfruit Icing

(each recipe serves 4–6 people)

Seafood Filo Pies
with Capsicum Sauce

1 packet filo pastry
100 grams melted butter
1 kilo fresh filleted fish – gurnard, snapper, or salmon, diced
salt and freshly ground black pepper
1 lemon

Brush 1 sheet of filo pastry with melted butter. Place another sheet on top and brush with butter. Repeat with two more sheets to make 4 sheets.

Cut filo in half down the middle.

Place a handful of diced fish on each piece of pastry, on the diagonal.

Season with salt and freshly ground black pepper, and a squeeze of lemon juice.

Fold up like a parcel. Repeat with remaining fish.

Brush tops with melted butter.

Bake at 200ºC for 10–25 minutes.

Capsicum Sauce

2 red capsicums, de-seeded and sliced
1 cup fish stock
2 tablespoons olive oil
2 tablespoons lemon juice
salt and freshly ground black pepper

Place the capsicums and stock in a saucepan.
Bring to the boil and simmer for 15 minutes.
Blend in a food processor. Return to the saucepan, bring back to the boil and add olive oil and lemon juice.
Season with salt and freshly ground black pepper.
To serve: drizzle *Capsicum Sauce* over *Seafood Filo Pies*.

Silverbeet, Apple and Parmesan Pie, *served with Aubergine and Tomato Sauce*

Pastry

2 cups flour
150 grams cold unsalted butter
½ teaspoon salt
125 grams sour cream

Combine the flour, salt and butter in a food processor.
  Pulse until the dough resembles fine breadcrumbs.
Add the sour cream and pulse until firm dough is formed.
Wrap in cling-film and leave to rest for 30 minutes.
Roll out ⅔ of the pastry to fit a 26 cm flan tin.
Roll out the remainder of the pastry to cover the top.

Filling

½ cup currants
½ cup raisins
2 bunches silverbeet leaves, sliced in strips
1 ½ cups Parmesan cheese, grated
½ cup pine nuts, lightly toasted
150 grams blue cheese, diced
2 eggs, lightly beaten
2 tablespoons olive oil
salt and freshly ground black pepper
1 Granny Smith apple, peeled, cored and sliced

(recipe cont'd next page)

Cover the currants and raisins with boiling water to soften. Set aside for 30 minutes.

Wash the silverbeet leaves. Add wet leaves to a large saucepan and simmer gently until wilted and lightly steamed.

Drain and press between two plates to remove the excess water. Transfer to a bowl.

Add the drained currants, raisins, grated Parmesan, pine nuts, blue cheese, eggs, olive oil, salt and pepper.

Spoon half the mixture into the pie shell, add the sliced apple in a single layer and top with the remaining filling.

Place the pastry top over the filling.

Bake at 190ºC for 35–40 minutes on fan bake until golden brown.

Serve hot or cold topped with *Aubergine and Tomato Sauce* (see following) and a simple green salad.

Aubergine and Tomato Sauce

1 red onion
2 cloves garlic, crushed
2 red chillies, de-seeded and sliced
2 tablespoons olive oil
250 grams small aubergines (or one large one), diced
500 grams very ripe tomatoes, skinned and chopped
1 teaspoon honey
handful of fresh basil
salt and freshly ground black pepper

Sauté the onion, garlic and chillies in olive oil until soft.
Add the chopped aubergines, chopped tomatoes and honey.
Simmer until the mixture is thick and reduced.
Add chopped basil, salt and pepper and stir through before serving.

Fresh Tuna *with Avocado and Diced Tomato Guacamole*

6 tuna steaks
2–3 tablespoons olive oil
sea salt and freshly ground black pepper

Place the tuna steaks in a flat baking dish. Rub with olive oil, salt and pepper.
Heat a frying pan and add the tuna steaks. Cook until the colour turns opaque ⅓ of the way up the side of the steak.
Turn over and cook until the colour turns opaque ⅓ of the way up again. The tuna must be rare in the middle.

Diced Tomato Guacamole

2 avocadoes
juice of 1 lemon
salt and freshly ground black pepper
1 tomato, halved, de-seeded and finely chopped

Remove the flesh from the avocadoes and place in a bowl. Add the lemon juice and salt and pepper. Mash with a fork until smooth.
Fold in diced tomato.
To serve: top tuna steaks with *Diced Tomato Guacamole* or a fruity salsa.

Grilled Tomatoes with Braised Red Onion, Red Capsicum and Florence Fennel

2 red capsicums, halved and de-seeded
6 large ripe tomatoes
2 tablespoons balsamic vinegar
2 tablespoons extra-virgin olive oil
sea salt and freshly ground black pepper
2 large red onions, thinly sliced
4 cloves garlic, crushed
2 small bulbs Florence fennel, sliced
handful chopped parsley

Grill the red capsicum halves, cut side down until the skin is blackened and bubbled.
Cover with a tea towel. When cool remove skin and slice lengthways. Set aside.
Cut the tomatoes in half through the middle.
Place in a baking dish (cut side up) and drizzle with balsamic vinegar and olive oil.
Season with salt and pepper.
Grill for 10–15 minutes until starting to look caramelised and crisp around the edges.
In a frying pan sauté the red onion slices and garlic until soft. Add the Florence fennel and capsicum slices. Panfry for 3–4 minutes.
Toss through chopped parsley. Season and serve on top of the grilled tomatoes.

Sweet Potato and Sage Ricotta Tart

500 grams fresh ricotta
1 cup grated Parmesan cheese
3 eggs
1 cup fresh rocket leaves
½ cup parsley, chopped
½ cup fresh sage leaves
½ teaspoon flaky sea salt
freshly ground black pepper
1 large kumara, peeled
2 tablespoons extra-virgin olive oil

Put the ricotta, Parmesan cheese and eggs in the food processor and blend until smooth.

Add the rocket, parsley and half of the sage and pulse until well combined.

Spoon mixture into a greased 20 cm spring-form cake tin.

Shave the kumara with a vegetable peeler into long ribbons and arrange on top of the tart.

Season with flaky sea salt and freshly ground black pepper.

Drizzle with a little extra-virgin olive oil.

Bake at 160ºC for 1 hour.

To serve: in a small saucepan heat the remaining oil and fry the sage leaves until crisp.

Remove the tart from the oven and pour the oil and sage mixture over the top.

Allow to cool to room temperature before removing from the tin.

Persimmon Cakes
with Passionfruit Icing

pulp from enough ripe persimmons to make 2 cups (about 3)
½ cup caster sugar
2 tablespoons lemon juice
100 grams butter
⅔ cup brown sugar
2 eggs, lightly beaten
1 ½ cups self raising flour
½ teaspoon cinnamon
pinch salt
2 tablespoons milk

Icing
1 ½ cups icing sugar
2 fresh passionfruit

In a saucepan combine the sugar, persimmon pulp and lemon juice. Bring to the boil and simmer until the mixture has reduced by half (to 1 cup). Cool.
In a bowl cream the butter and brown sugar, beat in the eggs one at a time.
Fold in the flour, cinnamon, salt, milk and persimmon pulp and stir until combined.
Spoon the batter into muffin tins. (Makes 1 dozen.)
Bake at 180ºC for 20–30 minutes or until firm to touch.

Icing
Sift the icing sugar into a bowl. Add the pulp of two passionfruit. (If the icing is too thin add more icing sugar one tablespoon at a time.) Spread icing with a knife onto the top of the persimmon cakes before serving.

Auckland Markets: Avondale – May

Visiting markets in our largest city and its regions emphasises the importance of being able to shop locally: having a good market close by, in a place of this size, is crucial for cutting down on travel time and expenses. The Auckland area provides many markets, not only in the city, but to the north in Matakana and in the south to Clevedon, with several others in between. As in many other regions throughout the country, more and more markets are opening up to satisfy the insatiable demand for fresh, seasonal, local produce.

The city of Auckland itself hosts numerous markets – some like La Cigale are now open on Saturdays and Wednesdays. La Cigale hosts a French style farmers' market and along with fresh local produce, it offers many imported products.

Ethnic communities are well-catered for at the South Auckland markets in Otara and Avondale – the latter market is held at the race course each Sunday morning. (I've been coming to this market for many years and have been known to get on the plane home again with vast bundles of lemon grass and bags of kaffir lime leaves and chillies.) It's hard to get a park close by, so shoppers walk from neighbouring areas pulling trolleys, pushing empty prams, or carrying boxes ready to be filled up with their week's purchases.

It is so interesting just sitting and watching what people have in their bags and trolleys. Some of the food here I haven't seen before: when I ask what to do

with it, I'm just told, 'It's for soup or stir fry.' There are mountains of attractive greens, bins of okra being expertly picked over by Indian women, fresh turmeric – yellow and white – ginger, and beautiful piles of bok choy, coriander, chokos and tables stacked with aromatic herbs. You can choose your own and buy as much as you want.

The Avondale market is a large, lively, busy, open air market which has always had a strong selection of Asian ingredients and caters for many ethnic communities. It opens very early and bursts into life every Sunday with a bustling crowd of young and old visiting the rows of stall holders in search of the best buys, while music blasts from a stereo somewhere. Many stalls also reverberate as the vendors bellow out the best price. As you work your way down each aisle – often stuck behind an old man pulling a very overloaded trolley – you become more and more drawn in by the atmosphere. Not all the food here is grown locally and quality is not always perfect, but there is always a lot to choose from.

Clearly my menu has an Asian feel, though I have given traditional ingredients my own interpretation, using aromatic flavours like lemon grass, kaffir lime leaves, ginger, garlic and chillies in a soup, finger food, main, vegetables and even dessert.

The slow-cooked pork belly slices are quite wonderful: served with the zucchini pancakes and vegetables, this dish is a firm favourite in our house.

Likewise the fun wonton cones – if you don't like the idea of making these shapes, you could always just roll the filling up into a parcel. (Recently while having our bathroom renovated, I was looking for something to serve the cones in for my class. My ingenious builder, Mervyn, transformed an old wooden batten from the ceiling by drilling holes into it, so it looked like the trays used to serve ice-cream at dairies. Magic!)

The inspiration for these steamed coconut puddings came from the fresh coconuts piled up at the market. (I love making use of fresh grated coconut: I think the hardest job for the uninitiated in this recipe is getting the coconut open. I've been known to drop coconuts on the concrete – but if you try this, and you've never used a fresh coconut before, make sure you drain the coconut milk out first!) I've suggested here that you serve these cakes with poached nashi pears, but kiwifruit, green and golden, or feijoas, persimmons or a salad including them all would be just as delicious.

There is such a huge and varied selection of produce available in this region: the best way to explore what's on offer is to visit your local markets.

AVONDALE MARKET, AUCKLAND

Spicy Zucchini Soup, served with Soba Noodle Salad

Spicy Diced Pork in Wonton Cones

Slow Baked Pork Belly Slices with Orange and Soy

Zucchini and Noodle Pancakes

Roasted Cauliflower and Asian Greens with a Warm Spicy Dressing

Steamed Coconut Puddings with Nashi Pears in Kaffir Lime and Palm Sugar Syrup

(each recipe serves 4–6 people)

Spicy Zucchini Soup
served with Soba Noodle Salad

2 tablespoons peanut oil
1 onion, sliced
1 leek, sliced
1 small fresh red chilli, finely chopped
½ teaspoon fresh ginger, grated
1 clove garlic, crushed
2 kaffir lime leaves, thinly sliced
1 stem fresh lemon grass, sliced
   (outer stems removed)
1 kilo zucchini, chopped
4 cups vegetable or chicken stock
1 tablespoon fish sauce
½ can coconut milk – 1 cup
2 tablespoons fresh coriander, chopped
salt and freshly ground black pepper

In a large saucepan heat the oil. Add the onion, leek, chilli, ginger, garlic, lime leaves, and lemon grass. Sauté for 4–5 minutes or until the onion is cooked and soft.
Add the zucchini and cook for a further 5 minutes.
Add the remaining ingredients except coriander and simmer until the zucchini is tender.
Add the chopped coriander.
Purée in batches and return to the saucepan. Season with salt and freshly ground black pepper.
To serve: ladle the zucchini soup into warm bowls and top with a tongful of *Soba Noodle Salad* (see above) and a sprinkling of chopped coriander.

Soba Noodle Salad

150 grams soba noodles
½ red onion, thinly sliced
4 spring onions, thinly sliced
   on the diagonal
1 red pepper, halved, de-seeded
   and thinly sliced
¼ cup coriander leaves, chopped
2 teaspoons fresh mint, finely chopped
1 tablespoon lemon juice
1 tablespoon kecap manis
salt and freshly ground black pepper

Cook the noodles in boiling salted water for 4–5 minutes or until tender.
Refresh in cold water. Drain.
In a bowl combine the noodles with the remaining ingredients.
Season with salt and freshly ground black pepper.
Cover and leave for 30 minutes.

Spicy Diced Pork
in Wonton Cones

1 kilo shoulder pork
½ cup sea salt
3 cm piece of fresh ginger
300 grams fresh green beans,
  thinly sliced
3 stalks celery, thinly sliced
1 cup peanuts, roasted
  and coarsely chopped
1 cup spring onions, thinly sliced

¼ cup peanut oil
1 fresh chilli, de-seeded
  and finely sliced
½ cup oyster sauce
¼ cup soy sauce
1 tablespoon sesame oil
1 tablespoon caster sugar
handful fresh coriander, chopped

Place the pork, ginger and sea salt in a large saucepan. Add enough cold water to cover and simmer for 30 minutes or until the pork is just cooked.

Drain the pork and refresh under cold water. Cut the excess fat from the pork and discard. Dice the meat into small pieces.

Combine the chilli, oyster sauce, soy sauce, sesame oil and caster sugar.

Heat a large frying pan on high and add 1–2 tablespoons of peanut oil.

Pile in the pork. Stir fry until the pork is browned.

Add the sliced beans, celery, spring onions and peanuts then the oyster sauce mixture.

Mix to combine and heat through. Transfer to a bowl. Toss through chopped coriander.

Serve pork in *Wonton Cones* (see following) or in iceberg lettuce cups.

Wonton Cones

11 cm metal cones (come in a pack of six – for creamed horns)
20 wonton wrappers
vegetable oil for frying

Wrap wonton wrappers around the metal cones. Seal the edges with a little water. Trim the tops.
Heat a small frying pan with 1 cm of oil. Shallow fry the cones in small batches. Turn to cook them evenly.
Drain on paper towels.
Repeat with remaining wonton wrappers.
To serve: fill with the pork mixture and serve immediately.

Slow Baked Pork Belly Slices
with Orange and Soy

1 kilo pork belly, cut into 10–12 thick strips
2 tablespoons vegetable oil
1 ½ cups beef stock
½ cup soy sauce
¼ cup mirin (sweet rice vinegar)
juice and zest of 1 orange
2.5 cm piece of ginger, sliced thinly
2 cloves garlic, sliced
2 fresh chillies (red or green), de-seeded and finely chopped
1 disk of palm sugar or 2 tablespoons brown sugar
1 cinnamon stick
2 tablespoons coriander, chopped

In a large frying pan heat the oil and sear the pork strips on each side, in batches, until brown.
Return all the strips to the pan and cover with water. Simmer for 20 minutes. Drain the poaching liquid.
Add the stock, soy sauce, mirin, orange juice and zest, ginger, garlic, chillies, sugar and cinnamon. If necessary add enough water to cover pork.
Bring to the boil. Cover and gently simmer for 1½ hours.
Transfer the pork strips to a baking dish.
Boil the stock uncovered for 20 minutes or until thick and syrupy.
Just before serving grill the pork strips on each side until they start to crisp.
To serve: place pork slices on the *Zucchini and Noodle Pancakes* (see following) with the reduced stock drizzled over the top. Sprinkle with chopped coriander.

Zucchini and Noodle Pancakes

80 grams vermicelli noodles
½ cup coconut milk
½ cup rice flour
2 zucchini, grated and squeezed to remove moisture
2 tablespoons fresh coriander, chopped
4 egg whites
salt and freshly ground black pepper
vegetable oil

Soak noodles in boiling water for 5 minutes. Drain.
In a medium sized bowl combine coconut milk and rice flour.
Add the drained noodles, grated zucchini and coriander.
Whisk the egg whites until they form soft peaks, and gently fold into the noodle and zucchini mixture.
Season with salt and freshly ground black pepper.
Heat ½ cm of oil in a frying pan. Cook a large spoonful of mixture until lightly golden on both sides. Repeat. Keep warm.
Serve topped with *Slow Baked Pork Belly Slices with Orange and Soy*.

Roasted Cauliflower and Asian Greens

with a Warm Spicy Dressing

1 cauliflower, cut into flowerets with stalks removed
4 tablespoons peanut oil
500 grams bok choy or a mixture of Asian greens (washed)
2 teaspoons ground coriander
2 teaspoons ground cumin
1 teaspoon paprika
2 cloves garlic, thinly sliced
juice of 1 lemon
2 tablespoons fresh coriander, chopped

Place the cauliflower in a baking dish. Drizzle with ½ the peanut oil and cover with tin foil. Roast for 30 minutes at 200ºC until the cauliflower is tender.

Wash the Asian greens thoroughly.

In a large frying pan lightly fry the ground coriander, cumin and paprika until fragrant. Add the remainder of the peanut oil and garlic. Cook very gently until the garlic is golden.

Pile the wet bok choy or Asian greens in pan with lemon juice. Toss until wilted. Add the cauliflower and heat through.

Serve sprinkled with chopped coriander.

Steamed Coconut Puddings *with*

Nashi Pears in Kaffir Lime and Palm Sugar Syrup

Pudding

175 grams unsalted butter
¾ cup caster sugar
1 teaspoon vanilla essence
3 eggs
1 ½ cups self raising flour
½ cup fresh coconut, grated
   (or ¾ cup dried shredded coconut)
⅓ cup coconut milk

Grease and line the bottoms of 8 x 125 ml ramekins.
Cream the butter and sugar until light and fluffy, whisk in the vanilla then the eggs one at a time.
Fold in the flour, grated coconut and coconut milk.
Spoon the mixture into the ramekins. Place ramekins in a baking dish.
Pour in enough hot water to come halfway up the sides of the ramekins.
Cover the baking dish with tinfoil. Bake at 180ºC for 30–35 minutes, until the puddings are well risen and firm to the touch.

Topping

1 cup fresh coconut, grated
  (or 2 cups dried shredded coconut)
¼ cup caster sugar
1 egg white

In a bowl combine the grated fresh coconut, caster sugar and egg white. Spread on a lined baking dish and bake at 180ºC for 15–20 minutes until lightly toasted. Toss with a fork 2–3 times during cooking. Cool.

Nashi Pear Syrup

175 grams palm sugar, grated
2 cups water
2 kaffir lime leaves, thinly sliced
2 medium nashi pears, peeled,
  halved and sliced

Combine the palm sugar and water in a saucepan. Heat gently until the sugar dissolves; add the kaffir lime leaves and pears.
Poach pears for 10–15 minutes or until tender. Remove the pears.
Bring the syrup to the boil and reduce by half.
To serve: turn out the coconut puddings onto serving plates. Top with the toasted coconut and 2–3 slices of pear. Spoon the syrup over the top.

The Otago Farmers' Market Dunedin – June and July

Visiting the Otago Farmers' Market on a clear, sunny Saturday morning in the middle of winter always gives me a great sense of achievement – apart from the fact that I managed to haul myself out of bed and park the car without losing my cool (this has to be the scene of the worst parking anywhere).

At this market you can fill your basket with inexpensive winter vegetables like carrots, cabbages, parsnips, leeks, cauliflower, brussels sprouts and yams: the market gives any household a wonderful choice of fresh vegetables for the week. Many of these vegetables thrive in the cooler conditions and need harsh frosts to sweeten their flavour. The Southland swede is a good example; if you drive down to Invercargill there are often many roadside stalls – sometimes consisting of just a wheelbarrow outside a gate – full of swedes.

Large pumpkins were a $1.00 each for many weeks over June and July – this versatile vegetable can stock everyone's kitchen all winter, for soups, pies, roasted vegetable platters and salads.

Apples and pears are available in a number of bins at the market, so that you can choose the variety you want: many sold locally are old favourites you might remember from childhood. They are often all the same price, so you can end up with a bagful of all varieties: a healthy version of pick 'n' mix.

Each week I see familiar faces – this market has become a meeting place for friends buying their breakfast, chatting over an espresso, and listening to the live music or the voice of Colin Dennison encouraging people to taste his cheese. It makes this a buzzy, busy place where some people come for entertainment, but many are just getting on with the business of buying.

The Dunedin market is extremely active and very successful. It doesn't seem to matter what time you go during the morning, it is always hard to find a park and often you have to queue, and juggle the fruits and vegetables you've chosen.

Frequently stall holders sell out – especially those offering marvellous bread, whole flounders for a dollar each, and the attractive, eye-opening purple broccoli.

Stall holders become friends with their customers and see them regularly each week; you can tell that the shoppers, too, have their favourite stalls – whether it be the woman from Central Otago with the pine nuts, hazelnuts and quinces, or the students with their shitake mushrooms. Organic produce features highly with vegetables, beef and lamb all available. Queen of the market has to be Linda from Havoc Pork. Now famous after being on 'Country Calendar', she is an inspiration and a goddess to all those who are followers of her pork products. She has one of those fantastic personalities that attracts, and makes people happy about using the market.

Thank goodness these guys are so busy and doing well: they deserve it, for getting up at some ghastly hour to be ready by opening time and, they hope, beating their first customers there.

In the winter month of June I have given the meals a North African feel.

The flavours of the Middle East are some of my personal favourites. Spices like cumin, coriander, turmeric, cinnamon, ginger and sumac all play a role in giving dishes intense depth and can be used in a huge variety of ways to create stunning recipes and meals.

Introducing new flavours and ingredients into your cooking helps to provide variety and diversity to weekly meals. Not only does it give you an appreciation of ethnic cooking styles, but if you have children, it helps to broaden their tastes and understanding of culinary traditions.

A good recipe to help you start exploring Middle Eastern cuisine is the amazing fritters, which consist mainly of feta cheese and spinach, and which are flavoured with cumin seeds. Truly moreish, they can be made into small portions as a finger food, or larger patties if served for lunch with a salad.

Rice and couscous are always preferred to potatoes at our house. I suggest buying your rice from a nearby Asian food store. You'll probably find that five kilograms come in a lovely cloth bag with a zip along the top – which is great for storing all sorts of things later.

Couscous is really just the smallest version of pasta: made from flour and egg, it's mixed then rubbed through the hands to create small grains. Traditionally, it's steamed in a lovely big steamer called a coucousier. I buy instant couscous – which, when covered with boiling water or stock, swells up in less than ten minutes. Fluff it with a fork, season with salt and pepper, and it's ready to use.

The addition of cooked vegetables, nuts and dried fruit can turn the couscous into a salad, a great vegetarian dish, or an accompaniment for tajines, and meat or fish dishes.

The Farmers' Market in Dunedin has a comprehensive selection of nuts during the winter months, most of which are grown in Central Otago. There are huge walnuts, hazelnuts, pine nuts, and for a shorter season, fresh chestnuts. Remember that nuts sold in their shells – like the ones at the market – will keep well in cool, dark storage for a year or more. However, once they have been opened they start to oxidise and become rancid in a relatively short time. Keep shelled nuts like walnuts, pine nuts and pistachios in the freezer – that way you can be sure they won't have the bitter, rancid flavour of old produce.

On a recent trip to Rome, I saw a Roman selling roasted chestnuts on the corner of the Spanish Steps. The chestnuts were roasted on a brazier and as they cracked open he filled paper cones with the scorching hot chestnuts. They cost quite a considerable amount if I remember rightly – but somehow at that moment a pile of hot, sweet, beautiful chestnuts was worth it; I can still remember the flavour. An excellent addition to the Dunedin Market on a cold winter's Saturday morning would be someone with a big drum, roasting chestnuts.

There is another taste of Europe at the market already, though: we are now seeing more and more local olive oil for sale. The olives are picked at the beginning of winter and pressed immediately. They

must be stored in dark bottles, so it's difficult to see the intense golden to green colours of this highly flavoured nutritious oil. I always encourage people in my classes to buy olive oil from all over New Zealand, and compare the flavours; many of us are very good at buying bottles of wine on our travels, but we should include olive oil, too. Use it for drizzling over perfectly ripe tomatoes or char-grilled vegetables and salads, or have an olive oil tasting session with your friends, using good, artisan bread.

Winter doesn't mean it's time to give up on salads and in this menu I have included three beauties – they came from a session I did at the Melbourne Food Festival a number of years ago, and I still like their simplicity. They use everyday ingredients and yet twist the flavours to provide three of my favourite winter salads.

Winter offers an abundance of sweet, flavoursome fruits and vegetables waiting to be accompanied by seafood, meats and cheeses. Long, slow cooking, hearty soups and winter greens for salads and fritters provide a multitude of choices – and the Otago Farmers' Market has a wonderful selection.

THE OTAGO FARMERS' MARKET, JUNE

Spinach and Feta Fritters

Tajine of Lamb Shanks,
served with Couscous and
Preserved Lemon

Tunisian Fish Tajine

Middle Eastern Salads:
Carrot and Harissa Salad,
Moroccan Honeyed Tomato Salad,
Coleslaw with Sumac and Pastrami

Orange and Almond Syrup Cake

(each recipe serves 4–6 people)

Spinach and Feta Fritters

150 grams mixed green salad leaves (mesclun, spinach or rocket)
2 spring onions or chives
150 grams Parmesan cheese, grated
150 grams feta cheese, crumbled
1 cup flour
2 eggs
2 teaspoons whole cumin seeds
2 teaspoons fresh thyme, finely chopped
salt and freshly ground black pepper
olive oil or vegetable oil for frying

Trim greens and chop coarsely. Thinly slice spring onions and add to the greens.
In a bowl combine cheeses, flour, thyme, cumin seeds and eggs.
Add the chopped greens and season to taste. Mix well.
In a frying pan heat about 1 cm oil.
Shallow fry tablespoonfuls of the batter, in batches, for 2–3 minutes. Flatten slightly and turn over until golden on both sides.
Drain on absorbent paper. Serve fritters immediately.

Tajine of Lamb Shanks
served with Couscous and Preserved Lemon

3–4 tablespoons vegetable oil
6 lamb shanks, trimmed of excess fat
2 onions, peeled and sliced thinly
5 cloves garlic, peeled and sliced
2 tablespoons ground coriander
2 tablespoons ground cumin
2 red chillies, de-seeded and sliced
5 cm piece of ginger, peeled and finely chopped
1 tablespoon turmeric
1 cinnamon stick
¼ cup honey
1 cup white wine
1 cup beef stock
15 pitted prunes, soaked in boiling water for 1 hour
1 handful of fresh coriander, chopped

In a heavy pan heat the oil and sauté the shanks until brown all over. Transfer to a deep baking dish or tajine.

In the same pan, sauté the onions and garlic until they begin to caramelise and soften.

Add the coriander, cumin, chillies, ginger, turmeric, cinnamon stick and honey.

Add the wine, beef stock and prunes, stir well. Pour over the shanks.

Cover with a lid or tin foil. Bake at 160ºC for 2½–3 hours, or until the meat falls off the bone.

When cooked, remove the shanks from the sauce. Cover with foil to keep them warm.

Skim the fat from the sauce and transfer the sauce to a saucepan. Boil until the liquid has reduced by half and has thickened.

Pour the sauce over the shanks, garnish with fresh coriander and serve with *Couscous and Preserved Lemon* (see following).

Couscous and Preserved Lemon

1 ½ cups couscous
2–3 cups heated chicken or vegetable stock
1 teaspoon salt
3 preserved lemons (see below)
¼ cup parsley, chopped
¼ cup coriander, chopped

In a large bowl cover the couscous with stock and leave for about 10 minutes until completely absorbed. Fluff up with a fork.
Remove the flesh from the lemons and discard. Wash and slice the lemon peel thinly. Add to the couscous.
Stir through the chopped parsley and coriander.
Serve with the *Tajine of Lamb Shanks*.

Preserved Lemons

250 grams plain salt	*2–3 cloves*
10 lemons	*1 stick cinnamon*
1 fresh bay leaf	*extra lemon juice*

Cut the lemons into quarters, but not all the way through.
Put a spoonful of the salt into the bottom of a sterilised jar.
Tip salt into a large bowl. Rub the salt into the skin of each lemon and push it into each quarter.
Pack lemons into the jar, inserting spices; press down hard on the fruit to release as much juice as possible.
Spoon over the remaining salt from the bowl. Cover with extra lemon juice.
Wipe the rim of the jar and cap the jar tightly.
Store in a cool place for 1 month before using.

Tunisian Fish Tajine

5–6 tablespoons olive oil
700 grams potatoes, peeled and cut into 1 cm cubes
1 teaspoon turmeric
2 medium onions, thinly sliced
1 stalk celery, thinly sliced
2 cloves garlic, crushed
2 fresh chillies, de-seeded and thinly sliced
4 teaspoons cumin
2 teaspoons paprika
pinch saffron, infused in 2 tablespoons warm water
2 x 400 gram tins whole tomatoes, chopped roughly
600 grams thick white fish – cod or groper
salt and freshly ground black pepper
large handful of fresh coriander, chopped

In a large frying pan, heat 2–3 tablespoons of olive oil. Add the potatoes and turmeric. Panfry, tossing to coat the potatoes with the oil.

Transfer to an oven dish and bake at 180°C for 20 minutes or until potatoes are cooked and starting to crisp.

Meanwhile in the frying pan sauté the onion and celery in 2 tablespoons of oil. When the onion starts to soften add the garlic, chillies, cumin, paprika and saffron.

Stir in the tomatoes and cook for a further 5 minutes. Season with salt and freshly ground black pepper.

As soon as the potatoes are cooked season the fish and place the fillets on top of the potatoes.

Spoon the tomato mixture over and around the fish fillets.

Return to the oven for 5–6 minutes to cook the fish.

Serve in large bowls, sprinkled with chopped coriander.

Carrot and Harissa Salad

1 kilo carrots
4 tablespoons olive oil
sea salt and freshly ground black pepper
1 clove garlic, crushed
2 tablespoons harissa (see following)
2 tablespoons white vinegar
½ cup black kalamata olives
2 tablespoons parsley, chopped
2 tablespoons fresh coriander, chopped

Peel carrots, cut into batons and place in a baking dish.
Toss in 2 tablespoons of olive oil. Season with sea salt and freshly ground black pepper.
Cover and bake for 45 minutes at 180ºC. Cool.
In a bowl mix together the garlic, *Harissa* and white vinegar. Slowly whisk in the remaining 2 tablespoons of olive oil.
Add the olives and chopped herbs to the carrots.
Toss the garlic and *Harissa* mixture through the carrots.
Transfer to a serving dish.

Harissa

1 roasted red capsicum
12 dried red chillies
1 teaspoon ground cumin seeds
½ teaspoon ground coriander
½ teaspoon caraway seeds
2 cloves garlic, crushed
sea salt to taste

Blend all ingredients in a food processor until smooth, and use as above.
Store in the fridge for up to one month.
(Warning! This is hot.)

Moroccan Honeyed Tomato Salad

12 large ripe tomatoes
½ cup olive oil
¼ cup honey
½ teaspoon salt
½ teaspoon freshly ground black pepper
½ cup sesame seeds, lightly toasted
2 tablespoons mint leaves, chopped

Dice the tomatoes into 1 cm cubes.
Warm the honey slightly and whisk in the olive oil.
Pour over the diced tomatoes and season with salt
    and freshly ground black pepper.
Allow to macerate for 15 minutes.
Mix through toasted sesame seeds and chopped fresh mint.
Transfer to a serving dish.

Coleslaw with Sumac and Pastrami

400 grams finely shredded cabbage
2 tablespoons fresh coriander, chopped
½ cup pine nuts, lightly roasted
½ cup sultanas
juice of 1 orange
½ red onion, finely chopped
100 grams shaved pastrami
¼ cup lemon juice
¼ cup olive oil
1 teaspoon sumac
sea salt and freshly ground black pepper

Soak the sultanas in the freshly squeezed orange juice for ½ hour.

In a large bowl combine the shredded cabbage, coriander, pine nuts, sultanas, juice, red onion and shaved pastrami.

In a small bowl whisk together the lemon juice, olive oil and sumac.

Pour over the shredded cabbage, toss to combine and leave to macerate for ½ hour before serving. Season with sea salt and freshly ground black pepper.

Transfer to a serving dish.

Orange and Almond Syrup Cake

2 medium oranges
200 grams unsalted butter
1 cup caster sugar
4 eggs
2 cups flour
1 cup ground almonds
½ cup sliced almonds
1 teaspoon baking soda
1 cup buttermilk
2 teaspoons vanilla essence

Syrup
1 cup sugar
½ cup orange juice
¼ cup water
2 tablespoons orange zest

Wash the oranges. Place in a saucepan. Cover with water and simmer for 1 hour.
Cool. Purée in a food processor until smooth.
Cream the butter and sugar until light and fluffy. Add the eggs one at a time and beat.
Fold in the flour, ground almonds, sliced almonds, baking soda, buttermilk, vanilla
    and finally the orange puree. Mix gently.
Spoon the mixture into a greased 26 cm ring-tin and bake at 180ºC for 45 minutes
    or until the cake is golden brown and bounces back when pressed.

Syrup
While the cake is baking, heat the sugar, orange juice,
    water and orange zest in a small saucepan.
Bring to the boil and simmer gently for 10 minutes.
Drizzle syrup over the warm cake.
Remove the cake from the tin when it's cool.

Dunedin – July

THE OTAGO FARMERS' MARKET, JULY

Artichoke, Parsnip and Apple Soup
with Porcini Mushrooms

Cheese and Walnut Biscuits

Shinbeef, Bacon and Mushroom Ragù

Parsnip, Leek and Parmesan Terrine

Roasted Pumpkin with Cashew Nuts
and Sesame Dressing

Spicy Roasted Yams with Sumac

Pear and Ginger Upside-down Cake

(each recipe serves 4–6 people)

Artichoke, Parsnip and Apple Soup with Porcini Mushrooms

10 grams dried porcini mushrooms
3–4 tablespoons olive oil
1 red onion, finely sliced
2 cloves garlic, crushed
1 kilo Jerusalem artichokes, peeled and chopped
3 parsnips, peeled and sliced
3 apples, peeled, cored and sliced
2 fresh bay leaves
2 litres chicken stock
3–4 tablespoons cream
salt and freshly ground black pepper
2–3 tablespoons parsley, chopped

Place the porcini mushrooms in a small bowl, add 300 ml of hot water. Leave to soak for about 30 minutes.
In a large saucepan, sauté the red onion in the oil and garlic until soft but not coloured.
Add the Jerusalem artichokes, parsnips, apples, bay leaves and stock.
Lift out the porcini mushrooms and add the strained soaking liquid to the vegetables.
Simmer for 20–30 minutes until the vegetables are soft. Blend in a food processor or use a stick blender.
Return the soup to the saucepan. Bring to the boil. Slice the porcini mushrooms finely, add to the soup along with the cream.
Season with salt and freshly ground black pepper and serve with a sprinkling of chopped parsley.

Cheese and Walnut Biscuits

2 cups flour
½ teaspoon baking powder
1 teaspoon salt
250 grams chilled unsalted butter, cubed

¼ cup freshly grated Parmesan cheese
1 ½ cups grated tasty cheese
2–3 tablespoons lemon juice
1 cup walnut halves

Place the flour, baking powder and salt into a food processor.
Add the butter and process until the mixture resembles coarse breadcrumbs.
Add the cheeses and pulse until combined.
Drizzle in the lemon juice, 1 tablespoon at a time, and pulse until the mixture forms a dough.
Transfer the mixture to a lightly floured bench and knead in the walnuts.
Divide the mixture in two and roll each piece of dough into a log, about 2–3 cm in diameter.
Wrap each log in baking paper and then in 2 layers of foil. Twist the ends to secure.
Refrigerate the cheese logs for 1 hour or until firm. (Logs can remain in the fridge for 3–4 days or can be frozen.)
Unwrap the logs and slice across in 5 mm rounds. Place disks on a lined oven tray and bake at 180ºC for about 15 minutes or until golden.
Cool on a wire rack before serving.

Shinbeef, Bacon and Mushroom Ragù

2 kilos beef (shinbeef with bone removed, or cross-cut blade)
250 grams thick sliced bacon, diced
2 onions, diced; or
    10 pickling onions
3 tablespoons flour
1 cup red wine
3 cups beef stock
2 tablespoons tomato paste
250 grams mushrooms, sliced or halved
1 tablespoon fresh rosemary, chopped
3–4 tablespoons vegetable oil
1 tablespoon redcurrant jelly
2 tablespoons parsley, chopped
salt and freshly ground back pepper

In a heavy based saucepan, sauté the bacon in oil until crisp. Drain on paper towels.
Cut the beef into 1 cm cubes. Sauté in batches until browned on all sides. Remove.
Add the onions to the saucepan, sauté until soft. Stir in the sliced mushrooms.
Return the bacon and beef to the onion mixture.
Add wine, stock, tomato paste and rosemary. Bring to the boil.
Transfer ragù to a casserole dish.
Bake at 160ºC until the meat is tender, about 2 hours.
Just before serving add redcurrant jelly and chopped parsley and season with salt and freshly ground black pepper.
Serve with the *Parsnip, Leek and Parmesan Terrine* (see page 103).

Parsnip, Leek and Parmesan Terrine

450 grams parsnips
2 leeks, cut lengthways
4 eggs
⅓ cup cream
1¼ cups freshly grated Parmesan cheese
¼ cup fresh thyme, chopped
salt and freshly ground black pepper

Boil the parsnips until they have softened. Cool a little. Cut into strips lengthways ½ cm wide.

Blanch the leeks in boiling water, then refresh in cold water.

Beat the eggs with the cream and Parmesan cheese. Season with salt and freshly ground black pepper.

Lay ⅓ of the parsnips on the bottom of a lined loaf tin or terrine dish, then layer ¼ of the leeks on top. Sprinkle with 1 tablespoon thyme and pour over ⅓ of the egg mixture.

Continue layering, finishing with a top layer of leeks.

Bake at 180ºC for 45 minutes.

Allow to rest for 10 minutes before turning out and slicing.

Roasted Pumpkin with Cashew Nuts and Sesame Dressing

1.5 kilo butternut or crown pumpkin, peeled and de-seeded
2 teaspoons flaky sea salt
freshly ground black pepper
2 tablespoons sesame oil
½ cup cashew nuts, toasted and roughly chopped
½ cup sesame seeds, toasted

Dressing
⅓ cup mirin (sweet rice vinegar)
⅓ cup lemon juice

Cut pumpkin into 8 even-sized long chunks. Season with salt and pepper and place in a baking dish.
Drizzle over sesame oil then pour in 1 cup boiling water.
Roast for 40–50 minutes at 180ºC, until cooked.
Place pumpkin in serving dish, add toasted cashew nuts.
Combine the dressing ingredients and pour over the pumpkin.
Sprinkle over the sesame seeds before serving.

Spicy Roasted Yams with Sumac

1 kilo yams
2–3 tablespoons vegetable oil
3 cloves garlic, crushed
3 teaspoons sumac
2 teaspoons paprika
½ teaspoon chilli powder

If your yams are small keep them whole otherwise cut them in half lengthways.
Place in a baking dish and toss with oil, crushed garlic and spices.
Roast for 30 minutes at 180ºC.
Pile onto a serving platter.

Sumac is a North African spice with sour, citrusy flavours.

Pear and Ginger Upside-down Cake

¼ cup caster sugar
2 cups water
juice of 1 lemon
4–5 pears, peeled, cored and halved
   (Taylor's Gold, Beurre Bosc)

Topping

125 grams butter
1 cup brown sugar

Gingerbread

2 cups flour
1 cup brown sugar
1 teaspoon baking soda
1 teaspoon baking powder
4 teaspoons ground ginger
½ teaspoon mixed spice
½ teaspoon nutmeg
1 teaspoon cinnamon
150 grams butter
1 cup golden syrup
2 eggs
1 cup milk

Place sugar, water and lemon juice in a saucepan. Bring to the boil.
Add the pears and simmer for 2–3 minutes or until just cooked. Cool.

Topping

Soften the butter in the microwave. Add the brown sugar and cream until light and fluffy.
Spread the topping onto the bottom of a 26 cm square or round spring-form cake tin.
Arrange the cooked pears cut side down.

Gingerbread

Sift the dry ingredients into a large bowl.
In a small saucepan melt the butter, and add the golden syrup. Heat until combined.
In a separate bowl, lightly beat the eggs together.
Add the butter mixture, beaten eggs and milk to the dry ingredients. Stir well to combine.
Pour mixture into the cake tin on top of the pears.
Bake at 150ºC for 1 ¼ hours or until a skewer comes out clean. Cool for 30 minutes before serving.
Serve at room temperature or cold.
Note: this is a sloppy mixture and can drip – place a dish under the cake tin if it is likely to leak.

Wellington Markets August and September

Markets in the Wellington region are growing in number, and they offer a diverse range of shopping styles and produce. Proximity to home is so important, and here, as in other parts of New Zealand, vendors are realising what a demand there is for fresh, regional produce.

A drive to Porirua on a Saturday morning gives you the choice of two markets. The Porirua Saturday Morning Community Market, in the town centre, starts by seven a.m. but moves on by ten-thirty a.m. in order to return the space to a car park. The market then moves to the Hutt area. After visiting the Porirua Market it's an easy drive around the road to the Moore Wilson Farmers' Fresh Market in Kenepuru Drive.

It was early in the morning when Bill and I visited Porirua, and once again we just followed the trail of people – some already leaving with heavy bags and full trolleys. It was evident that this busy market was where families and locals bought their food requirements for the week.

Music seemed to drift around the car park yet the local religious group still made themselves very well heard above the buzz of shoppers.

This market had the largest range of seafood I'd seen at any market on our travels. The seafood stall was popular and crowded, and the selection ranged from crabs and kina to huge whole groper, snapper and moki. Fresh squid was certainly in hot demand and the young woman behind the counter was kept extremely busy. Shoppers were filling bags ready to be weighed and were waiting patiently to be served.

Shopping here was fun, and the group from Lions, who seemed to do all the supervision, did a grand job – constantly talking to people and making sure the stall holders were paid up and following the rules.

Porirua Market truly impressed, with its mountains of high quality, fresh spinach and bok choy and the baskets of cheaply priced broccoli, cauliflowers and watercress. The vegetables looked stunning – especially the rows of colourful lettuces. This market reminded me of the many markets in Italy that I visit on my tours, where markets have been the preferred shopping venue for hundreds of years.

It was pleasing to see families shopping together. I overheard one woman asking her two girls to choose the fruit they wanted for the week. I thought this was a fantastic idea – if your children get to choose the variety they like, it guarantees they'll eat it.

The beginning of August is a hard time of year. Winter seems to still be breathing at our backs, and yet the spring flush is just out of reach. Moore Wilson Farmers' Fresh Market was held under cover. Shopping here might not have had the vivaciousness of the vegetable stalls earlier in the morning, but the smart surroundings and the quality of the stalls definitely had their own appeal. Many sold products already prepared such as pesto, flavoured nuts and Turkish delight. The fresh shitake mushrooms were

beautiful; I am always inspired by people like the vendors at these stalls. They often start their business as a small cottage industry and it then grows with demand.

Wellington city itself has a couple of markets on a Sunday morning and we spent an hour on a glorious sunny morning, at the market venue just beside Te Papa overlooking the harbour. What a fabulous site. I think I recognised some of the vegetable dealers from Porirua the previous morning, but included here was new season's fresh asparagus – irresistible to take home to Dunedin, especially when we don't see our local crop in the south for another couple of weeks.

The busy Porirua and Wellington markets inspired me to give the August menu an Italian flavour. Simple inexpensive arancine (rice balls) are always delicious and popular with everyone. They are often served as a snack or lunch dish – yet are quite substantial. The arborio rice encases a filling of a simple ragù and a small cube of melting mozzarella cheese. After watching a demonstration in Messina, Sicily, I now dip the rice balls in a thin batter of flour and water and then coat them in breadcrumbs before shallow frying, which gives them a nice crisp finish.

I have included wonderful chickpea bread here – basically it is just chickpea flour and water with a little salt and chopped parsley. However, once it is fried and crisp, it's very appetising. Panelle is a traditional North African recipe, also often served in Palermo, Sicily, where it's frequently cooked at the markets and eaten hot as a snack.

The pork chop recipe is mouth-watering. Rubbed with olive oil and chopped rosemary, the chops are pan-fried then baked with apples, fennel and grapes. I then finish them off with a drizzle of tart apple syrup and grill them.

The biscuits are also Sicilian-inspired and are moreish and tasty. These biscuits use almonds and are flavoured with lemons and oranges. At home after a meal we rarely have dessert, but a luscious biscuit with a cup of coffee will meet that occasional sweet craving.

In the September menu I've used seafood, spinach, mushrooms and rhubarb – which were all in such plentiful supply.

The pancakes are filled with a mixture of mushrooms but they make fantastic wraps for a variety of vegetables, meat and fish. It's a good idea to purchase a good, heavy-based pancake pan – and remember to leave the pancake batter to rest for 30 minutes or so before you use it. This makes the pancakes easier to cook.

WELLINGTON MARKETS, AUGUST

Chickpea Panelle (Fritters) with Green Olive Pesto

Arancine – Rice Balls with Beef Ragù

Sicilian Meatballs with Lemon and Bay Leaves

Grilled Polenta topped with Mushrooms and Olives, served with a Roasted Vegetable Sauce

Pork Chops baked with Apples, Fennel and Grapes

Lemon and Almond Biscuits

Orange and Almond Biscuits

(each recipe serves 4–6 people)

Chickpea Panelle (Fritters)
with Green Olive Pesto

2 cups chickpea flour, sifted
2 ½ cups cold water
1 teaspoon salt
¼ cup parsley, finely chopped
vegetable oil for shallow frying

Add cold water to a heavy-based saucepan; pour in the chickpea flour in a steady stream, whisking briskly to avoid any lumps.

Add the salt and parsley and cook over a medium heat, stirring constantly until the mixture is thick and pulls away from the sides of the pan.

Pour the mixture onto a cold surface or a wooden board, and using a spatula spread it out to about ½ cm thick. Leave to cool.

Cut the panelle into squares (4 cm) and then into small triangles.

Heat oil in a frying pan and shallow-fry fritters in batches until golden brown.

To serve: sprinkle with salt and a squeeze of lemon juice and eat at once or top with *Green Olive Pesto* (see following).

Green Olive Pesto

½ cup extra-virgin olive oil
6 anchovies
2 tablespoons capers
5–6 mint leaves
1 cup stuffed green olives
freshly ground black pepper

In a food processor combine the olive oil, anchovies, capers and mint.

Add the olives and pulse to combine. The mixture needs to be moist and spreadable, but still to have texture.

Season with freshly ground black pepper.

Arancine – Rice Balls with Beef Ragù

Ragù

1 onion, finely chopped
2 cloves garlic, crushed
4 tablespoons vegetable oil
200 grams minced beef
200 grams minced pork
100 grams minced chicken
½ cup white wine
1 cup beef stock
2 tablespoons tomato paste
salt and freshly ground
    black pepper
handful parsley, chopped

Rice

2 cups Arborio rice
1 teaspoon salt
½ teaspoon saffron strands
    (about 6 threads)
50 grams butter
½ cup Parmesan cheese, freshly grated
50 grams mozzarella cheese, cubed

Coating

1 cup flour
water
dried breadcrumbs
vegetable oil for frying

Ragù

Sauté the onion and garlic in the oil until soft.
Add the minced meats and cook until they are browned and all the liquid has reduced.
Add the white wine, beef stock and tomato paste. Simmer until liquid has reduced and thickened.
Add chopped parsley and season.
Cool.

Rice

In a large saucepan, add the rice, 1 ½ litres water, salt and saffron.
Bring to the boil and simmer for 10–15 minutes, until the rice is tender.

(recipe cont'd next page)

Leave the lid on and rest for 10 minutes.

Stir in the butter and Parmesan cheese and leave the rice to cool.

In a separate bowl whisk together flour and enough water to make a thin batter.

Moisten one hand and scoop up a handful of rice. Flatten it slightly across your other palm. Spoon in a little of the ragù and press it into the middle of the rice. Add a cube of the mozzarella cheese.

Take some more rice and fold it over the filling. Mould the rice to form a ball.

Dip the arancine in the batter then in the dried breadcrumbs.

Chill for 15–30 minutes. Shallow fry in batches until golden.

Bake for 10 minutes at 180ºC and serve.

Sicilian Meatballs with Lemon and Bay Leaves

500 grams minced pork
1 cup pecorino or Parmesan cheese, freshly grated
1 cup dried breadcrumbs
⅓ cup parsley, chopped
zest of 1 lemon
½ teaspoon salt
2 eggs
vegetable oil
2 cups white wine
8 bay leaves
zest and juice of 1 lemon

In a large bowl place the minced pork, grated cheese, breadcrumbs, parsley, lemon zest and salt.

Add the eggs and mix together, either with a wooden spoon, or I like to use my hands (wearing gloves).

Form the mixture into small balls (golf ball size) – wet your hands to make it easier.

Heat a thin layer of oil in a frying pan – large enough to take the meatballs without over-crowding. Fry on a medium heat for about 10 minutes, until nicely browned on all sides. Shake the pan a little to make sure they are not sticking.

Add the white wine. Pour in just enough hot water to cover the meatballs. Add the bay leaves and leave to simmer until the sauce is well reduced and starting to become syrupy.

Add the lemon juice and zest. Check seasoning. Cook for a few minutes more.

Serve with *Grilled Polenta topped with Mushrooms and Olives* (see following) or with fresh pasta.

Grilled Polenta topped with Mushrooms and Olives,
served with a Roasted Vegetable Sauce

Polenta

2 cups water
2 cups milk
1 teaspoon salt
200 grams fine instant polenta
1 cup Parmesan cheese, freshly grated
3–4 tablespoons olive oil
2 cloves garlic, crushed

In a large saucepan bring the water, milk and salt to the boil.
Pour in the polenta, slowly in a steady stream, constantly stirring with a wooden spoon.
Lower the heat and continue stirring until the polenta starts to come away from the sides of the saucepan, approx 5–8 minutes.
Remove the pan from the heat. Stir in half the Parmesan cheese.
Pour the mixture onto a board or baking sheet, and spread it out to about 5 mm thick.
Allow the polenta to cool and set.
Cut the polenta into squares (4 cm). Place in a baking dish, overlapping the squares slightly.
Combine the olive oil and crushed garlic. Drizzle over the top of the polenta. Sprinkle with the remaining cheese and grill for 5–6 minutes, until the polenta is crisp and golden on top.
Serve topped with *Mushrooms and Olives* and *Roasted Vegetable Sauce* (see following).

Mushrooms and Olives

1 kilo mushrooms – Swiss brown, button, oyster or shitake, trimmed and halved
1 tablespoon fresh thyme, chopped
1 cup black kalamata olives
¼ cup olive oil
sea salt and freshly ground black pepper
handful of parsley, chopped

Place the mushrooms in a shallow baking dish and toss through the thyme, olives and olive oil. Season with salt and freshly ground black pepper.
Bake at 220ºC for 20–25 minutes, until the mushroom juices have evaporated.
Add parsley and stir.

Roasted Vegetable Sauce

200 grams mushrooms, halved
2 onions, peeled and quartered
4 carrots, cut into 5
2 cloves garlic
4 stems parsley
2 sprigs thyme
2 tablespoons olive oil
1 bay leaf
1.5 litres water
½ 440 gram tin tomatoes
½ cup white wine
1 teaspoon salt
2 tablespoons butter
2 tablespoons flour
salt and freshly ground black pepper

Place the vegetables and herbs in a baking dish and toss with the oil.

Bake at 220ºC for 30 minutes until the vegetables are golden.

Transfer the vegetables to a stock pot. Deglaze the baking dish with the white wine, and add to the saucepan with the water, tomatoes and salt.

Bring to the boil and simmer for 1–2 hours.

Pour the stock through a sieve, pressing down firmly to extract all the juices before discarding the vegetables.

To make the sauce: melt butter in a saucepan. Add the flour and cook the roux until bubbling. Add the vegetable stock and bring to the boil, stirring constantly. Season.

Drizzle sauce over *Grilled Polenta topped with Mushrooms and Olives*.

Pork Chops baked with Apples, Fennel and Grapes

6 pork chops
2–3 tablespoons vegetable oil
2 stems of fresh rosemary, finely chopped
1 cup white wine
2 apples, peeled, cored and sliced
1 bulb fennel, thinly sliced
2 cups green grapes
¼ cup 'Gusto Apple Syrup'
coarse sea salt and freshly ground black pepper

In a small bowl combine the chopped rosemary and vegetable oil. Rub into the pork chops and leave at room temperature for 1 hour.
Heat a heavy-based frying pan. Sauté the pork chops until golden and browned on both sides. Transfer to a shallow baking dish.
Deglaze the pan with the white wine and pour over the pork chops.
Place slices of apple and fennel on the pork chops and top with grapes.
Season with coarse sea salt and freshly ground black pepper. Cover with tinfoil.
Bake at 180ºC for 40–50 minutes.
Remove the baking dish from the oven and take off the tinfoil.
Drizzle over the apple syrup and grill until bubbling and golden.
Serve with the *Grilled Polenta topped with Mushrooms and Olives* (see page 118).

Lemon and Almond Biscuits

1 ½ cups ground almonds (very fine)
1 cup caster sugar
½ teaspoon ground cinnamon
zest of 1 lemon
2 egg whites

Combine the ground almonds in a bowl with the caster sugar. Add cinnamon and lemon zest.
In a separate bowl beat the egg whites until soft peaks form. Fold into the almond mixture. Mix well.
Place teaspoonfuls of mixture on a lined baking sheet.
Bake for 10–15 minutes at 180ºC until the ridges start to brown.
Cool on a wire rack. Store in an airtight container.
Makes approx 20 biscuits.

Orange and Almond Biscuits

5 egg whites
1 cup caster sugar
⅓ cup honey
1 cup flour
3 ½ cups sliced almonds
1 cup crystallised orange peel

Place all the ingredients in a large saucepan.
Stirring constantly, cook over a low heat until the sugar starts to dissolve and you can smell the sugar.
Using wet hands roll the mixture into balls. Flatten slightly and place on a lined baking sheet.
Bake at 200ºC until crisp and golden.
Makes approx 25 biscuits.

Wellington – September

WELLINGTON MARKETS, SEPTEMBER

Baked Seafood and Nori Rolls, served with Avocado and Hazelnut Salsa

Veal Schnitzel Rolls with Lemon, Caper and Celery Stuffing, served with Redcurrant Sauce

Roasted Potatoes with a Spicy Tomato Sauce

Warm Spinach Salad

Mushroom-Filled Pancakes with Spinach Sauce and Sweet Balsamic Syrup

Rhubarb and Walnut Cake

(each recipe serves 4–6 people)

Baked Seafood and Nori Rolls, *served with Avocado and Hazelnut Salsa*

125 grams scallops or crab meat
1 egg white
pinch of chilli powder
2 tablespoons cream
salt and freshly ground black pepper

250 grams blue cod
2 egg whites
pinch of chilli powder
⅓ cup cream
salt and freshly ground black pepper

200 grams sliced smoked salmon
9 sheets of nori

In a food processor lightly purée the scallops, egg whites, chilli powder and cream. Season with salt and pepper. Transfer to a bowl and refrigerate for 30–40 minutes.
Repeat with the blue cod.
Place a sheet of nori on a sushi roll mat. Spread ⅓ of the scallop mixture over the nori sheet. Roll firmly into a cylinder. Repeat two more times with remainder of filling.
Place another sheet of nori on the mat and cover with 5–6 slices of smoked salmon. Place the rolled scallop roll on one

edge and roll the salmon around the scallop cylinder. Repeat with other two rolls.

Spread another sheet of nori with ⅓ of the blue cod mousse. Place the salmon and scallop roll at one edge and roll up. Repeat this process to make 3 rolls.

Wrap each roll in tin foil. Twist the ends and bake at 180ºC for 10–15 minutes.

Remove the rolls from the foil, slice and serve hot or cold with *Avocado and Hazelnut Salsa* (see following).

Avocado and Hazelnut Salsa

flesh of 1 avocado
⅓ cup hazelnuts, roasted, skinned and roughly ground
1 teaspoon horseradish sauce
juice of 1 lemon
salt and freshly ground black pepper

In a food processor pulse all the ingredients together until just combined.

Veal Schnitzel Rolls with Lemon, Caper and Celery Stuffing,
served with Redcurrant Sauce

2 tablespoons vegetable oil
1 onion, peeled and diced
3 sticks celery, thinly sliced
¼ cup sultanas
¼ cup capers
zest of 1 lemon
3 anchovy fillets, chopped
1 teaspoon celery seeds
4 slices good white bread
1 egg
½ teaspoon salt
freshly ground black pepper
6 slices veal schnitzel
olive oil

In a frying pan sauté onion and celery slices in vegetable oil until soft.
Add sultanas, capers, lemon zest, anchovies and celery seeds and combine. Set aside.
Cut the crusts from the bread. Slice bread into small cubes.
Stir the cubed bread through onion mixture. Add egg and seasoning.
Divide the stuffing between veal schnitzels, and roll meat into a roll. Secure with a toothpick.
Dust each veal roll in flour.
Pan fry in a little olive oil, until evenly browned and cooked through.
Serve with *Redcurrant Sauce* (see following).

Redcurrant Sauce

½ cup red wine
½ cup beef stock
⅓ cup redcurrant jelly

Deglaze the meat pan with red wine and beef stock and boil until reduced by half. Add redcurrant jelly. When melted add ⅓ cup cream and simmer until thick.

Roasted Potatoes
with a Spicy Tomato Sauce

1 kilo potatoes unpeeled and cut into
   1 cm cubes (Van Rosa or Agria)
olive oil
salt and freshly ground black pepper

Spicy Tomato Sauce

1 onion, peeled and finely diced
2 cloves garlic, crushed
2 x 440 gram tins whole
   peeled tomatoes
1 tablespoon tomato paste
½ cup white wine
1 teaspoon chilli sauce
4 fresh bay leaves
½ teaspoon fresh thyme
1 teaspoon sugar
½ cup parsley, chopped
¼ cup fresh basil, chopped
½ cup Parmesan cheese, freshly
   grated

In a large baking dish toss the potatoes in 2–3 tablespoons of olive oil. Season with salt and pepper. Make sure the potatoes are in a single layer. Bake at 200ºC for 30–40 minutes until golden and crisp.

Spicy Tomato Sauce
In a shallow saucepan sauté the onion and garlic in a little olive oil until soft.
Add the remaining ingredients except parsley and basil. Simmer gently for 20–30 minutes until mixture thickens.
Transfer to a food processor and purée until smooth. Season with salt and pepper. Stir through chopped parsley and basil.
Place the warm potatoes on a serving dish and pour the re-heated *Spicy Tomato Sauce* over the top.
Serve with freshly grated Parmesan cheese and more chopped parsley.

Warm Spinach Salad

2 cups fresh basil (approx 1 large bunch)
6 cups fresh spinach leaves, washed and trimmed
1 cup cubed bread, crusts removed
½ cup olive oil
3 cloves garlic, crushed
125 grams belly bacon strips, sliced
½ cup pine nuts
salt and freshly ground black pepper
75 grams shaved Parmesan cheese

Toss spinach and basil together.
In a baking dish toss bread cubes in 3–4 tablespoons olive oil.
  Bake at 200ºC until crisp and golden.
In a frying pan heat the rest of the oil gently over a medium heat.
  Add garlic and bacon and toss until cooked.
Stir in the pine nuts and sauté until nuts begin to brown.
In a large serving dish toss spinach and basil with the warm
  bacon dressing, toasted bread and shaved Parmesan.
  Serve immediately.

Mushroom-Filled Pancakes with
Spinach Sauce and Sweet Balsamic Syrup

Pancakes

1 cup flour
2 eggs
1 ½ cups milk
5 fresh basil leaves
½ cup Parmesan cheese, freshly grated
salt and freshly ground black pepper

Mushrooms

3–4 cups sliced mushrooms (oyster, shitake, brown or button)
2 tablespoons olive oil
3 cloves garlic, crushed
1 teaspoon fresh thyme, chopped
1 cup semi-dried tomatoes
salt and freshly ground black pepper

In a food processor combine the flour and eggs; add enough milk to make a batter the consistency of pouring cream.
Pulse in the fresh basil leaves and grated Parmesan cheese. Season.
Pour into a jug and leave to rest for 20 minutes.
Pour a ladle of batter into a greased, heavy-based frying pan. Tip the pan to coat the bottom and make a thin pancake – like a crêpe.
Cook until the bottom is just brown; turn over and cook the other side.
Repeat, and stack the cooked pancakes on a plate one on top of another.

Sauté mushrooms in olive oil with garlic and fresh thyme until cooked.
Add semi-dried tomatoes. Season.

Spinach Sauce

4 spring onions
200 grams spinach, washed and trimmed
1 cup vegetable stock
5 basil leaves
2 tablespoons olive oil
salt and freshly ground black pepper

Sauté onions in a little olive oil, add spinach and toss until wilted.
Transfer to food processor and blend with vegetable stock and basil. Drizzle in the olive oil slowly and blend. Season.

(recipe cont'd next page)

Sweet Balsamic Syrup

½ cup sugar
½ cup water
½ cup balsamic vinegar

Combine sugar and water in a saucepan.
  Simmer until consistency is syrupy.
Add the balsamic vinegar and simmer until
  reduced by half.

To assemble pancakes

½ cup sundried tomatoes, chopped
½ cup Parmesan cheese, freshly grated

Spoon a pile of mushrooms onto each pancake.
  Fold in the sides and roll up. Place filled pancake
  rolls in a greased baking dish.
Pour over *Spinach Sauce*, and drizzle with
  Sweet Balsamic Syrup.
Sprinkle top with chopped sundried tomatoes and
  Parmesan cheese.
Bake at 200ºC until golden and heated through
  (approx 20 minutes).

Rhubarb and Walnut Cake

4 sticks rhubarb
1 ½ cups sugar
2 ½ cups flour
1 ½ teaspoons baking soda
1 ½ teaspoons cinnamon
1 ½ teaspoons allspice
½ teaspoon salt
1 ½ cups walnuts, roughly chopped
2 eggs
200 grams melted butter

Slice rhubarb and mix with the sugar.
In a separate bowl, combine flour, soda, spices and salt. Stir through the chopped walnuts.
Beat the eggs into the slightly cooled melted butter. Fold the rhubarb and sugar into the egg and butter mixture. Mix gently into the dry ingredients.
Spoon into a greased 24 cm spring-form ring tin.
Bake at 180ºC for 40–45 minutes.

Hawkes Bay Markets – October and November

Napier has a small covered market providing a selection of fresh fruit and vegetables. When we visited, new season's asparagus, beautiful jams and jellies and fresh homemade bread were also on offer. Although small by comparison to many other markets, it fills a niche, and obviously has its regulars who rely on its proximity to Napier city. It doesn't have the ambience of other markets, but it would be cool and shady in the heat of summer.

In contrast, the Black Barn Growers' Market in Hawkes Bay is all ambience – small, friendly and busy. Built in the Black Barn Vineyard, close to their underground cellars, it forms a circle under a ring of plane trees, and loops around the coffee stall and its inevitable queue. The coffee stall was obviously the centre of the morning's social outing, with many young people pushing toddlers in prams, couples anxious to fill their shopping bags with fresh vegetables, beautiful avocadoes, and the fresh bread on offer, which sold out quickly.

Many stalls sold ready-to-go preserves – from chutneys and relishes to jams and jellies, using locally grown limes, other citrus, fruits and vegetables.

I loved the Indonesian stall, which sold their own sweet kecap manis, satay sauce and sambals. These I use in marinades and sauces for barbecue meals during the summer.

This popular destination market is in a beautiful situation – set amongst rows of grape vines that run along the Black Barn bistro and a beautiful outdoor theatre. The theatre is used during the summer for movies, and tickets were sold at the market.

Nestled behind the central Hastings streets on Sunday mornings, the Hawkes Bay Market sets up on the showgrounds, surrounded by mature trees. It offers quality products to locals who faithfully come each week to buy, socialise, listen to the great music and take advantage of the spur of the moment purchases this and every market encourages. I get the feeling many of the people at this market are here not just to shop but to take in the atmosphere, meet their friends, chat – and what better place to do it?

The market's circuit, full of tempting aromas and colourful sights, is like a promenade, as shoppers walk around, sussing out what they want to buy and sorting out the best purchases – the only detour being around the coffee queue. (What market would be without one?)

When you visit, taste the cheese from Hohepa Farm, the salami and smoked goods from the Deli, and olive products from Telegraph Hill. The market has everything covered from meat and venison to fruit and vegetables – the first of the new season's asparagus (sold by the same girls we saw in Napier the day before) – many varieties of extra-virgin olive oil, mushrooms, eggs, cheese and bread.

Even early in the spring season the market is able to provide shoppers with a marvellous selection of fresh seasonal produce for meals throughout the week. This is a lively market and its size means there

is lots of room for dancing children and people picnicking and if your shopping gets out of control, you can borrow a wheelbarrow.

As in Napier, many stalls and food producers are selling a variety of ready-to-go sauces, jams and chutneys made from their products, including chillies and limes. Olives and tomatoes are dried, brined and packed in many ways by the clever Telegraph Hill people; I can also heartily recommend their wonderful Sweet Cabernet Drizzle, which I've used in the caramelised onion recipe that follows.

My menu for October has used all the purchases I made on my morning at the Hawkes Bay Market (except the chicken). I could have done with that wheelbarrow!

Planning salads – especially the asparagus recipe with shitake mushrooms, Florence fennel, olives, smoked beef and coriander all dressed with local extra-virgin olive oil – gives me a huge amount of satisfaction. I love combining flavours and textures that result in a stunning one dish meal, or a side serving that can accompany a cooked chicken. As a result I have dedicated the recipes in November to one dish salads – meals that can be eaten by themselves or accompanied with fresh, homemade bread. These recipes are suitable for lunch or dinner.

I make the focaccia in this menu often, and certainly every day when I am on holiday. It's really very easy and takes minimal time. When I get up in the morning, I combine the yeast, water and sugar, eat my breakfast, and by then it's foaming and fluffy. I then add the flour, salt and olive oil, mix it all into a dough, knead it for five to six minutes, then put it back into the bowl. Just before I require it I finish off the recipe. It's a good idea when on holiday to find out where you can find some fresh rosemary.

Salad ingredients can be used in so many ways. I have combined them with meats and seafood to illustrate how effective and simple this type of meal can be. Often using a variety of ingredients can be perfect for people cooking for two or for themselves.

Making use of extras like hummus, pesto, tzatziki and mayonnaise will help spike up your salad and give it the wow factor. (These ingredients are so handy to have in the fridge all the time, and they're so useful in sandwiches for school lunches or snacks with baked pita bread.) This is another opportunity to make use of those wonderful extra-virgin olive oils we can buy throughout New Zealand markets now. (It's nearly Christmas and they make the perfect gift.)

These salads will serve you well throughout the year and can be used for outdoor eating or for lunch in the winter – just change the vegetables to suit the season, e.g. the roasted vegetable salad could be served hot during the winter with fresh or smoked salmon.

HAWKES BAY MARKETS, OCTOBER

Asparagus and Rice Tart

Salt-Baked Chicken, served with Walnut, Capsicum and Cumin Sauce

Dry-Roasted Potatoes topped with Caramelised Onions

Warm Mushroom Salad

Asparagus Salad with Fennel, Artichokes, Olives and Smoked Beef

Lime, Hazelnut and Chocolate Cream Pie

(each recipe serves 4–6 people)

Asparagus and Rice Tart

Pastry

2 cups flour
125 grams unsalted butter

500 grams asparagus (2 bunches)
⅓ cup Arborio rice
1 onion, finely chopped
2 cloves garlic, crushed
2 tablespoons olive oil
¼ cup Parmesan cheese, freshly grated
¼ cup Havarti cheese, freshly grated
3 eggs
½ cup cream
zest of 1 lemon
¼ cup parsley, chopped
salt and freshly ground black pepper
2–3 tablespoons extra-virgin olive oil

Process flour and butter in a food processor. Gradually add 2–3 tablespoons cold water until the dough forms a ball. Wrap dough in cling-film. Chill for 30 minutes.
Roll out the pastry to fit a 24 cm round or rectangular tart tin. Chill again for 15 minutes.
Line the pie shell with baking paper and fill with baking beans. Bake at 200ºC for 15 minutes. Remove the paper and beans. Cool.
Blanch the asparagus in boiling water for 1 minute. Refresh under cold water to cool quickly. Drain.
Cook rice in boiling salted water for 8 minutes. Drain and cool.
Sauté the onion and garlic in olive oil until soft. Transfer to a bowl and add rice, Parmesan, Havarti, eggs, cream, lemon zest and parsley. Season.
Pour rice mixture into the tart shell. Trim the asparagus to fit and place side by side on top of the rice. Brush the asparagus with olive oil. Bake at 180ºC for 20–25 minutes. Serve at room temperature.

Salt-Baked Chicken, served with Walnut, Capsicum and Cumin Sauce

Pastry
1 kilo coarse cooking salt
1 kilo flour
800 mls water

2 small free-range chickens
zest of 2 lemons
½ cup fresh sage leaves
½ cup fresh thyme leaves
6 cloves of garlic
6 tablespoons olive oil

In a food processor make the pastry in two batches. Process ½ the flour and ½ the salt together, and with the motor running, add half the water. Remove the pastry and knead it on a floured board until it comes together; wrap it in cling-film and rest for 30 minutes. Repeat.

In a food processor pulse the lemon zest together with the herbs, garlic and oil (or use a mortar and pestle.) Season.

Rub the lemon mixture over and inside the chickens. Slice the remaining lemons and place in each chicken cavity.

Preheat the oven to 200ºC.

Roll the dough into an oblong shape making it slightly thicker in the middle.

Place the chicken on the dough breast-side down and fold the pastry over the chicken encasing it completely. Make sure the dough is air-tight and there are no holes. Repeat with the remaining chicken.

Place the chickens in a baking dish. Bake for 1 hour. (The crust will go hard and the chicken juices will remain inside.)

(recipe cont'd next page)

Remove the chickens from the oven and leave to rest for 30–40 minutes.

To serve: crack open the pastry cases and discard. Joint the chickens and place on a serving dish.

You will end up with lovely, flavourful, moist chicken!

Walnut, Capsicum and Cumin Sauce

½ cup walnuts
1 red capsicum, halved, de-seeded and roasted
1 slice good white bread, crust removed, diced
½ teaspoon dried chilli flakes
1 teaspoon ground cumin
3 tablespoons pomegranate molasses
¼ cup extra-virgin olive oil

Place all the ingredients in a food processor and process until they form a firm paste.

Serve with *Salt-Baked Chicken* or as an accompaniment to grilled lamb or fish, or as a spread with flat bread.

Dry-Roasted Potatoes topped with Caramelised Onions

6–8 potatoes, chopped into chunks

4 red onions, sliced
2 brown onions, sliced
2 bulbs of fennel, sliced (optional)
8 cloves of garlic, peeled and chopped
4 stems fresh rosemary
zest and juice of 1 lemon
¼ cup Cabernet Drizzle (Telegraph Hill)
¼ cup balsamic vinegar
sea salt and freshly ground black pepper

Steam the potatoes until almost cooked.
Transfer to a baking dish and bake for 1 hour at 180ºC until crisp.

In a lined baking dish place the sliced onions, fennel, chopped garlic and rosemary.
Mix together the lemon zest and juice, Cabernet Drizzle, balsamic vinegar and 2 tablespoons water. Pour mixture over the onions and fennel and toss together.
Cover with tin foil and bake at 180ºC for 30–40 minutes.
Remove tin foil. Season with 1 teaspoon of sea salt and freshly ground black pepper.
Increase the heat to 200ºC. Bake for a further 10 minutes until starting to crisp.
Serve the potatoes on a platter topped with the caramelised onions.

Telegraph Hill's Cabernet Drizzle is a thick, sweet wine vinegar.

Warm Mushroom Salad

4 slices good bread, crusts removed and cut into 1 cm cubes
1 yellow capsicum, de-seeded and halved
200 grams brown mushrooms
200 grams button mushrooms
100 grams oyster mushrooms
2 shallots, thinly sliced
2 tablespoons thyme, chopped
2 tablespoons chives, chopped
2 tablespoons balsamic vinegar
2 cups mesclun salad mix
1 cup Gouda cheese, freshly shaved
⅓ cup extra-virgin olive oil (approx)
salt and freshly ground black pepper

Toss bread cubes in a little extra-virgin olive oil and bake at 200ºC for 10–15 minutes or until croutons are golden.

Grill the capsicum until blistered and black. Cover with a tea towel to cool. Remove the skin and slice.

Cut large mushrooms in half. Heat ¼ cup olive oil in large frying pan or wok. Sauté the shallots for 2 minutes. Add all the mushrooms and toss for 2–3 minutes or until they begin to soften. Add the herbs and balsamic vinegar and season.

Place mesclun salad in a large serving dish. Add the mushroom mixture and scatter with capsicum slices, shaved Gouda and croutons.

Drizzle with a little extra-virgin olive oil, and serve immediately.

Asparagus Salad with Fennel, Artichokes, Olives and Smoked Beef

500 grams asparagus (2 bunches)
1 bulb Florence fennel, sliced very thinly
½ cup artichoke hearts (in a jar)
1 cup Ugly Olives (Telegraph Hill)
2–3 tablespoons Hawkes Bay Extra-Virgin Olive Oil
100 grams sliced smoked beef (from the deli)
200 grams Parmesan cheese, freshly shaved
½ cup parsley, chopped

Blanch the asparagus in boiling salted water for 1 minute. Refresh under cold water. Drain.
In a bowl combine the Florence fennel, artichoke hearts and Ugly Olives.
Toss in 2 tablespoons of Hawkes Bay Extra-Virgin Olive Oil.
Pile asparagus on a serving platter. Top with the fennel mixture. Drizzle over remaining oil.
Sprinkle smoked beef and shaved Parmesan over salad and top with chopped parsley. Serve.

Telegraph Hill's delicious Ugly Olives are first dried and then marinated.

Lime, Hazelnut and Chocolate Cream Pie

Pastry

1½ cups flour
2 tablespoons ground hazelnuts
2 tablespoons icing sugar
150 grams cold butter, cut into cubes
1 egg yolk

Filling

1¾ cups milk
1 vanilla bean, split lengthwise
3 large egg yolks
½ cup caster sugar
⅓ cup flour
150 grams dark chocolate, broken into pieces
zest of 2 limes

Pastry

Process flour, hazelnuts, icing sugar and butter in a food processor. Add the egg yolk and slowly add 1–2 tablespoons cold water, pulsing until the mixture comes together in a ball.
Divide dough into 2 and wrap in cling-film.
Chill for 30 minutes.

Filling

In a small saucepan heat the milk and vanilla bean, until almost boiling. Remove from the heat and leave for 5 minutes to allow the flavour to develop. Remove the vanilla bean.
In a bowl whisk the egg yolks and sugar. Stir in the flour, then slowly pour in the milk while continuing to whisk.

Sit the bowl on top of a saucepan of boiling water. Stir the custard until it thickens and coats the back of a wooden spoon.

Divide the mixture between 2 bowls. Add the chocolate pieces to one and stir until melted and smooth. Add the lime zest to the other bowl of custard. Cool to room temperature.

Roll out one piece of pastry and line the bottom of a 24 cm flan dish.

Place spoonfuls of the chocolate custard around the outside edge of the pastry case, then spoon the lime mixture into the middle. Brush the edge of the pastry with a little water.

Roll out the remaining pastry and place over the top of the flan.

Trim and crimp the edges and slash 2–3 slits in the top of the pastry.

Bake at 180ºC for 30–35 minutes or until golden. Cool tart to room temperature.

Dust with icing sugar and serve.

Hawkes Bay Markets – November

HAWKES BAY MARKETS, NOVEMBER (SALAD PLATTERS)

Smoked Chicken Salad with Sundried Tomatoes, Olives and Feta

Lamb Souvlaki topped with Cucumber Tzatziki, served with Spinach Orzo Salad

Roasted Vegetable Salad with Sumac-Crusted Salmon, served with Horseradish Rouille

Venison Slices with Pearl Couscous Salad, served with Hummus and Basil Pesto

Focaccia Bread

Strawberry Flan with Crème Patissèrie

(each recipe serves 4–6 people)

Smoked Chicken Salad with Sundried Tomatoes, Olives and Feta

1 smoked chicken breast
½ cup sundried tomatoes
1 cup blanched almonds
2 cups mesclun salad mix
½ cup black kalamata olives
250 grams feta
3–4 tablespoons extra-virgin olive oil
1 tablespoon balsamic vinegar
flaky sea salt and freshly ground black pepper
½ cup parsley, chopped

Thinly slice the smoked chicken breast. Slice sundried tomatoes in four.
Dry-roast the almonds at 180ºC until starting to colour. Cool.
Dice the feta cheese in cubes.
In a large flat serving dish, layer all the salad ingredients.
Mix together the extra-virgin olive oil and balsamic vinegar. Drizzle over the salad and toss lightly.
Season and sprinkle with chopped parsley.

Lamb Souvlaki *topped with Cucumber Tzatziki, served with Spinach Orzo Salad*

1 kilogram lamb fillets or backstraps
¼ cup olive oil
1 tablespoon dried oregano
3 cloves garlic, crushed
1 teaspoon sea salt and freshly ground black pepper

Place the lamb in a flat dish.
Coat with olive oil, dried oregano, garlic, salt and pepper.
Cover and refrigerate for 1–2 hours.
In a frying pan or barbecue chargrill the lamb for 4–5 minutes each side, or until medium rare.
Leave to rest for 5 minutes before slicing.

Tzatziki

250 grams thick natural yoghurt
⅓ cucumber, halved lengthways, de-seeded and grated
1 clove garlic, crushed
½ cup fresh mint, chopped
1 tablespoon lemon juice

Combine all the ingredients of the tzatziki in a bowl.
Season with salt and freshly ground black pepper.
Refrigerate until required.

Orzo Salad

350 grams Orzo or Risoni (rice shaped pasta)
¼ cup extra-virgin olive oil
500 grams spinach (trimmed and washed)
⅓ cup fresh dill, chopped
4 spring onions, thinly sliced
½ baby cos lettuce, thinly sliced
1 cup flat leaf parsley, chopped
2 tablespoons basil leaves, chopped
¼ cup lemon juice
salt and freshly ground black pepper

In a large saucepan of boiling salted water cook the Orzo until al dente (approx 8–10 minutes). Drain, then rinse under cold running water to cool. Drain again.
Place Orzo in a bowl and toss through the olive oil.
In a frying pan heat 1–2 tablespoons olive oil. Add the washed spinach and toss until wilted.
Coarsely chop the spinach and add to the Orzo with the remaining ingredients. Season.
Serve with *Lamb Souvlaki* and *Cucumber Tzatziki*.

Roasted Vegetable Salad

with Sumac-Crusted Salmon, served with Horseradish Rouille

1 red capsicum
1 yellow capsicum
1 large aubergine, diced
2 zucchini, cut into quarters
1 large red onion, sliced
olive oil
salt and freshly ground black pepper

Cut capsicums in half, de-seed and grill until the skins are blistered and black. Place a tea towel over the top and cool. Rub off blackened skin, slice each half into 4, lengthways.
Pile the capsicums, aubergine, zucchini and red onion in a baking dish. Toss in a little olive oil.
Bake at 200ºC for 20–25 minutes. Cool.
Arrange all the vegetables on a large platter. Season.
Serve with *Sumac-Crusted Salmon* and *Horseradish Rouille* (see following).

Sumac-Crusted Salmon

1 side of salmon (approx 1 kilo), boned
1 tablespoon sumac
3–4 tablespoons olive oil

Cut the salmon into 6 slices. Transfer to a lined baking dish.
Sprinkle with sumac and olive oil.
Grill for 6–8 minutes until the salmon is just cooked.
Serve the salmon pieces with the salad.

Horseradish Rouille

2 cloves garlic, crushed
*2 thick slices white bread, crusts removed
   and soaked in ¼ cup milk*
2 tablespoons prepared horseradish
1 egg yolk
½ cup olive oil
salt and freshly ground black pepper

Put the first four ingredients in a food processor and purée.
Gradually add the olive oil in a thin stream. Season.

Venison Slices with Pearl Couscous Salad,
served with Hummus and Basil Pesto

500 grams venison (denver leg)
½ cup polenta

Cut the venison into two and roll in the polenta.
Heat 2–3 tablespoons vegetable oil. Pan fry venison until golden.
Transfer to the oven and bake at 180ºC for 8–10 minutes.
Rest for 5 minutes before slicing.

Pearl Couscous Salad

2 cups pearl couscous – Moghrabiah
2 ripe tomatoes, de-seeded and finely chopped
½ cup kalamata olives, pitted and quartered
½ cup parsley, chopped

Vinaigrette

⅓ cup olive oil
2 tablespoons lemon juice
2 tablespoons balsamic vinegar

Cook the pearl couscous in a saucepan of boiling, salted water until tender.
Drain and run under cold water to cool. Leave to drain.
In a bowl combine couscous, tomatoes, olives, parsley and vinaigrette.
Transfer to a serving dish and serve with slices of venison (or lamb, beef, chicken or fish) topped with *Hummus* and *Basil Pesto* (see following).
Or fill pita pockets with couscous salad and pan-fried tuna and top with *Hummus* and *Basil Pesto*.

Hummus

2 cups cooked chickpeas
2 cloves garlic
juice of 1 lemon
½ cup olive oil
sea salt and freshly ground
 black pepper

In a food processor place the chickpeas, garlic and lemon juice. Process until well blended.
Slowly drizzle in the olive oil. Blend. If the hummus is too thick add 3–4 tablespoons of boiling water. Season.

Basil Pesto

2 cups basil leaves
2 cloves garlic, crushed
4 tablespoons pine nuts
½ teaspoon salt
1 cup olive oil
⅓ cup Parmesan cheese, freshly grated

Combine basil, garlic and pine nuts in a food processor. Blend until smooth. Add salt, olive oil and Parmesan cheese and pulse to combine. Transfer to a jar and store in the refrigerator.

Focaccia Bread

2 x 7 gram sachets dried yeast
1 tablespoon sugar
650 mls warm water
6 cups strong flour – "00 farina"
1 tablespoon salt
3 tablespoons extra-virgin olive oil
1 cup extra flour

2 stems fresh rosemary, leaves removed
1 tablespoon flaky sea salt
extra-virgin olive oil

In a small bowl combine the yeast, sugar and water. Mix with a fork and leave until frothy (a few minutes).
In a large bowl add the first measurement of flour and salt. Make a well in the centre and pour in the frothy yeast mixture and olive oil.
Using a fork and a circular movement, slowly bring in the flour from the edges.
Continue mixing until the dough firms. Using your hands, pat the dough into a ball.
Tip the dough onto the bench and knead for 10 minutes (approx) or until it is springy and soft (you may need the extra flour).
Clean out the bowl, grease with a little oil and place the dough in the bottom.
Cover with cling-film and leave to rise in a warm place until it has doubled in size.
Roll the dough out to 1.5 cm thick and place it in a baking tray or roasting dish.
Leave to rest for 5 minutes.
Dimple the surface with your fingertips. Drizzle with extra-virgin olive oil. Sprinkle with rosemary leaves and salt.
Bake at 200ºC for 10–15 minutes or until golden on top.

Fine strong flour (00 farina) is especially suited to flatbreads and pizza dough as it easily develops gluten and gives the dough lots of elasticity.

Strawberry Flan with Crème Patissèrie

Pastry

2 cups flour
125 grams butter
¼ cup icing sugar
1 egg yolk
1–2 tablespoons water

Crème Patissèrie

2 cups milk
3 eggs
6 tablespoons flour
2 tablespoons cornflour
½ cup caster sugar
zest and juice of 1 orange

2 punnets strawberries, hulled and halved
½ cup redcurrant jelly

Pastry

Put flour, icing sugar and butter in food processor. Pulse to combine.
Add egg yolk and water – 1 tablespoon at a time – until the dough forms a ball.
Roll out to fit 26–28 cm flan dish. Chill for 10–15 minutes.
Bake blind in a hot oven until golden brown, 8–10 minutes.

Crème Patissèrie

Bring milk to the boil.
In a bowl combine eggs, flours and sugar, whisk until combined.
Slowly add the hot milk to the egg mixture whisking briskly.
Transfer custard back to the saucepan. Slowly bring to the boil, stirring constantly until thickened. Stir in the orange zest and juice.
Transfer crème patissèrie to a bowl. Cover and cool.

To assemble

Spoon crème patissèrie into pastry case.
Place strawberries on top of the crème filling in concentric circles.
Brush with warm, melted redcurrant jelly to glaze.

Otago Farmers' Christmas Market – December

The Christmas Farmers' Market in Dunedin has become a must over the years for all those people who like to provide the very best of local ingredients for Christmas dinner. Most years the stall holders come together for an extra market, depending of course on when Christmas Day falls. Otago and Dunedin residents are lucky to have this very special market; everything is here to ensure their Christmas and holiday meals are delicious, interesting, and made of the finest and freshest local produce.

Christmas Day in 2006 was on a Monday: perfect for all those people who could finish work and travel to family and friends over the weekend. Market Day remained on Saturday morning, except for a business like Havoc Pork, which had so many orders they had to make a special trip the day before and use a separate drop-off point to distribute the huge numbers of ham orders.

This is one market day of the year where arriving early is essential. Strawberries and local Jersey Benne potatoes were sold out by eight a.m. The queues of people anxious to buy fresh vegetables and fruit – especially the new season's cherries fresh from Central Otago – wound all the way around the stalls. Mountains of brightly coloured radishes sparkled in the sunlight, along with baskets of broad beans, carrots, white turnips and peas. It's always a treat to find the more unusual fruits like gooseberries and redcurrants. I love stewed fruit, like redcurrants and blackcurrants, gooseberries and rhubarb. I usually cook up a bowlful and keep it in the fridge, each morning adding a few spoonfuls to my homemade muesli, and finishing it off with yoghurt.

Christmas morning breakfast is a special tradition in our family and the market has a full range of choices for this meal: fresh fruit, bacon, ham, sausages, eggs, Jersey Benne potatoes that can be cooked and fried, bread, and fresh coffee, or a range of teas, plus the traditional Italian panettone from Indigo Bakery. (I also use their ciabatta for the turkey stuffing, and it makes great toast.)

It's hard to make fast progress around a market like this without stopping and meeting all your friends and acquaintances – wishing them a Merry Christmas and peeking into their bags to see what they have bought.

At the Christmas Market, buskers seemed to be everywhere, creating an amazing blend of music. The espresso coffee machines constantly churned out takeaway coffees, and many people were obviously eating their breakfasts. The crêpe stall was incredibly busy: the chef only looked up briefly to take the next order. I think this is a ritual Saturday morning breakfast for many market shoppers.

Another ritual of this market should be to make sure you don't go home without a selection of Evansdale cheese, and maybe some chocolate truffles and dried Central Otago fruits. It is Christmas after all and providing stunning food is what you do.

I have designed a very traditional Christmas dinner menu. I have tweaked it to include the flavours I like and modified each recipe so it can easily be prepared in advance to help take the stress out of a busy Christmas Day. (The comments I receive most often when demonstrating this menu is how useful it is to be able to do so much beforehand, and then just 'cook the menu off' on the day itself.) This menu can be used to feed two or three or any large gathering.

The shrimp cocktail is my interpretation of the 1970s version that was served in a glass and topped with Thousand Island dressing. Although I have kept to tradition and served the prawns on a bed of the essential shredded iceberg lettuce, mine uses the delicious Tom Yum paste which can be found in any Asian food store. It's hot and spicy and perfect with the prawns. I've also used the fresh flavours of mango, tomato and pickled cucumber to finish it off. The seafood stalls at this market only sell fresh fish, but the prawns I used were frozen: if you're local, Aaron at the Harbour Fish stall has them in his shops.

If you butterfly the turkey and cook the stuffing separately, the cooking time will be shorter than usual for this Christmas favourite. I have deliberately chosen a 3 kilogram turkey – originally I used this size so I could cook it in time to fit in with my Christmas cookery demonstrations. However, as they are small and always tender, I now prefer to use them. If I'm feeding a large crowd, I just buy two or three in preference to buying a larger turkey.

The potatoes in this menu are quite delicious. I have used fresh sage leaves to stuff each potato and baked them with fresh garlic, olive oil and crusty sea salt. (Don't be tempted to buy prepared garlic in a jar. It doesn't compare to freshly crushed garlic. Garlic is a brilliant bulb, each clove encased in its own paper to maintain freshness and flavour. If stored in a cool dark place it will last for a year. Even better than buying it is to grow your own. The rule is plant each clove on the shortest day and harvest on the longest. The plants are economical on space and it's rewarding to have 20 to 30 bulbs to use throughout the year.)

The vegetable bundles here can be assembled using any seasonal vegetables on hand. In December the last of the asparagus is still around along with new season's beans, carrots and white turnips. Later in the year I may well be inspired to use pumpkin, parsnips and yams, following the same recipe.

Instead of precooking these vegetables, as I do with the potatoes, I just blanch them in boiling water, toss them in a pan with a little maple syrup and balsamic vinegar, then wrap a selection of them in bacon. They can then be covered, chilled and cooked later in a hot oven – enough to heat the vegetables through and crisp the bacon.

It's hard not to include red berries in a dessert at this time of year. A beautiful bowl, filled to the brim with strawberries, raspberries or boysenberries, seems to define a New Zealand Christmas dessert.

This very rich hazelnut meringue recipe is the perfect accompaniment to those berries – a crisp, nutty meringue filled with chocolate mousse and Christmas fruit mince. Again the meringue and mousse can be prepared the day before, wrapped and stored – perfect if you have to travel, as you can put it together in five minutes when you arrive.

OTAGO FARMERS' CHRISTMAS MARKET

Prawn Cocktail served with Mango Salsa and Sweet and Sour Cucumber Slices

Butterflied Turkey with Fig and Bacon Crumble

Sage Roasted Potatoes

Roasted Vegetable Parcels

Hazelnut Meringue Layers with Chocolate Mousse and Fruit Mince

Panforte

(each recipe serves 4–6 people)

Prawn Cocktail *served with Mango Salsa and Sweet and Sour Cucumber Slices*

1 kilo raw prawns, shelled
¼ cup water
2 tablespoons fish sauce
3 tablespoons lemon juice
2 tablespoons fresh lemon grass, finely chopped
1 tablespoon kaffir lime leaves, finely chopped
4 tablespoons Tom Yum paste
1 spring onion, sliced
2 tablespoons fresh coriander, finely chopped
2 tablespoons fresh mint leaves, finely chopped
1 iceberg lettuce, thinly shredded

In a large frying pan, place the water, fish sauce, lemon juice, lemon grass, lime leaves and Tom Yum paste. Stir and bring to the boil, add the prawns. Cook until the prawns have changed colour.

Stir in the spring onion, coriander and mint leaves. Toss gently and cool slightly.

Mango Salsa

1 fresh mango, peeled and diced
1 ripe tomato, diced
2 tablespoons sweet chilli sauce or capsicum sauce
2 tablespoons lemon juice

In a bowl toss the salsa ingredients together.

Sweet and Sour Cucumber Slices

1 cucumber, halved, de-seeded and thinly sliced
1 tablespoon salt
3 tablespoons white vinegar
3 tablespoons sugar

Combine all ingredients in a bowl and marinate for 10–15 minutes. Drain.

Serve on a long platter or in individual glasses. Place the shredded lettuce on the bottom and spoon over the prawns and sauce. Top with the *Mango Salsa* (see above) and scatter the *Sweet and Sour Cucumber Slices* (see above) over the salsa.   This is a magnificent starter!

Butterflied Turkey with Fig and Bacon Crumble

1 x 3 kilo turkey (free range)
2 handfuls of fresh marjoram
6 cloves garlic, crushed
¼ cup extra-virgin olive oil
1 tablespoon sea salt
freshly ground black pepper

Cut the turkey down the breast bone and spread out. Place on a baking dish.
Tuck the marjoram underneath the turkey.
Cut a few slits into the turkey meat. Mix together the garlic, olive oil, sea salt and pepper, and rub mixture over the turkey skin and into the cuts.
Cover with tin foil and bake at 180ºC for 1½–2 hours.
Remove from the oven. Transfer to an oven-proof serving dish.
Pile the *Fig and Bacon Crumble* (see following) on top.
Bake uncovered for a further 15 minutes at 200ºC.
Leave to rest for 15–20 minutes before serving.

Fig and Bacon Crumble

½ cup port
2 cups dried figs, diced
½ cup dried cherries
¼ cup olive oil
1 onion, finely chopped
1 clove garlic, crushed
½ cup pine nuts
200 grams Havoc bacon, diced (or streaky bacon)
½ cup parsley, chopped
zest of 2 lemons
6 cups focaccia bread chopped into 1 cm cubes
1 cup chicken stock
salt and freshly ground black pepper
extra-virgin olive oil

In a saucepan heat the port. Add the figs and cherries. Leave to soak for 20–30 minutes.
In a frying pan sauté the onion and garlic in the olive oil until very soft.
Add the pine nuts, diced bacon, parsley and lemon zest and continue to cook.
Place the diced bread in a large bowl. Add the onion and bacon mixture and combine.
Pour over the chicken stock, and add the figs and port mixture. Season.
Transfer to an oven-proof dish and bake at 180ºC for 30 minutes.
Drizzle with a little extra-virgin olive oil.

Sage Roasted Potatoes

24 small Jersey Benne potatoes, scrubbed
24 sage leaves
extra-virgin olive oil
3 cloves garlic
sea salt and freshly ground black pepper

Bring a large saucepan of salted water to the boil. Add the potatoes and simmer until just cooked.

Place the potatoes on a lined baking sheet. Cut a deep incision in each (not all the way through). Insert a sage leaf.

Mix together the crushed garlic and olive oil. Brush liberally over the tops of the potatoes. Season.

Bake at 200ºC for 20–30 minutes.

Roasted Vegetable Parcels

300 grams fresh green beans
6 carrots
6 zucchini
2 tablespoons maple syrup
2 tablespoons balsamic vinegar
12 sprigs fresh thyme
12 slices streaky bacon
olive oil

Cut the carrots and zucchini into thick batons.
Blanch the vegetables in a pot of boiling water until just al dente. Drain.
In a frying pan add the maple syrup and balsamic vinegar. Heat gently until mixture starts to caramelise. Add the vegetables and toss until well coated.
Pile the vegetables into bundles of 6–8 pieces, add a sprig of thyme to each and wrap each bundle with streaky bacon.
Lay the bundles on a baking sheet. Pour over remainder of the maple syrup mixture.
Brush with olive oil. Bake at 250ºC for 5–8 minutes.
Makes 12 bundles.

These parcels can be made well in advance – chill in the fridge, then bake and serve.

Hazelnut Meringue Layers with Chocolate Mousse and Fruit Mince

6 egg whites
1 ½ cups caster sugar
2 tablespoons cornflour
2 teaspoons cocoa powder, sifted
1 cup hazelnuts, roasted, skinned and chopped

Beat the egg whites until stiff. Whisk in 2 tablespoons of the sugar.
Using a metal spoon fold in the remaining sugar – about a quarter at a time.
Fold in the cornflour then swirl in the cocoa powder to give a ripple effect.
Draw 3 circles on baking paper – 26 cm in diameter each.
Run the baking paper under the tap and give it a shake. Place on baking tray.
Spread the meringue mixture evenly over each circle.
Sprinkle the hazelnuts evenly over each layer.
Bake at 140ºC for 1 hour. Turn the oven off and leave to cool in the oven for a further 30 minutes.
Gently peel the baking paper from the meringues. Set aside.

Chocolate Mousse

125 grams dark chocolate –
   70% cocoa solids
4 tablespoons cream cheese
⅓ cup caster sugar
1 egg yolk

1 ¼ cups cream,
   whipped into soft peaks
1 ½ cups Fruit Mince
   (see below)

Place the chocolate in a china bowl and melt in microwave on low heat or over a bowl of boiling water.
In a separate bowl, beat the cream cheese, sugar and egg yolk until smooth.
Slowly pour in the melted chocolate and blend until combined.
Fold in the whipped cream and *Fruit Mince*.
Cover and chill for 1–2 hours or overnight.

Fruit Mince

1 cup sultanas
1 cup currants
1 cup raisins
½ cup dates

½ cup dried apricots, chopped
3 tablespoons brown sugar
1 small apple, grated
⅓ cup brandy

Pulse the dried fruit in a food processor until coarsely chopped.
Transfer to a bowl, add the remaining ingredients and toss to combine.
Store in a jar in the fridge. (Can be kept for 12 months.)

This will be more than you need for the cake, but great for mince pies.

(recipe cont'd next page)

To assemble the cake:

Place the first layer of meringue on a serving plate nut side down.

Spread with ½ the *Chocolate Mousse* and *Fruit Mince*. Place the next meringue layer on top nut side up. Spread with the remaining chocolate and fruit mixture.

Place the final layer on top nut side up. Press down very gently.

Leave in a cool place until ready to serve.

Dust with icing sugar and serve with fresh berries.

Panforte

1 cup hazelnuts, roasted and skinned
1 cup slivered almonds
⅓ cup glacé cherries
⅓ cup glacé pawpaw
⅓ cup dried apricots

⅓ cup candied peel
2 tablespoons cocoa
1 cup flour
½ cup caster sugar
½ cup liquid honey
⅓ cup dark chocolate

Combine hazelnuts, almonds, cherries, pawpaw, apricots, candied peel, cocoa and flour in a bowl. Mix well.

In a saucepan combine the caster sugar and honey. Bring to the boil and stir until the sugar has dissolved. Add the chocolate pieces and stir until melted.

Pour the honey mixture into the nut mixture and mix well. Knead with your hands to combine ingredients.

Press the dough into a 20 cm lined, loose-bottom flan pan.

Bake at 160ºC for 30 minutes.

Cool. Cut into thin wedges to serve.

Make Panforte in small flan dishes – perfect for Christmas gifts.

Index

Almond Biscuits, Lemon & 121
Almond Biscuits, Orange & 122
Almond, Orange &, Syrup Cake 96
Arancine – Rice Balls with Beef Ragù 114
Artichoke, Parsnip & Apple Soup 99
Asian Greens 79
asparagus 137, 138, 145
Asparagus & Rice Tart 137, 138
Asparagus Salad 145
Aubergine & Tomato Sauce 60
Aubergine, Tomato & Gruyère Torte 35
Avocado & Hazelnut Salsa 124

Baked Seafood & Nori Rolls 124
Balsamic Syrup, Sweet 131
Basil Pesto 154
beef
    Arancine – Rice Balls with Beef Ragù 114
    Shinbeef, Bacon & Mushroom Ragù 101
Beetroot, Roasted with Red Onions 36
biscuits
    Cheese & Walnut Biscuits 100
    Lemon & Almond Biscuits 121
    Orange & Almond Biscuits 122
Blueberry Sour Cream Cake 38
Bread, Focaccia 157
Butterflied Leg of Lamb 48
Butterflied Turkey 166

cakes
    Blueberry Sour Cream Cake 38
    Orange & Almond Syrup Cake 96
    Panforte 172
    Pear & Ginger Upside-down Cake 106
    Pear & Hazelnut Crumble Cake 52
    Persimmon Cakes with Passionfruit Icing 67
    Rhubarb & Walnut Cake 133

Caramelised Onions 141
Carrot & Harissa Salad 93
Cauliflower, Roasted & Asian Greens 79
Cheese & Walnut Biscuits 100
chicken
    Chicken Jerk 17
    Salt-Baked Chicken 139
    Smoked Chicken Salad 149
Chickpea Panelle (Fritters) 113
Chocolate Cream Pie, Lime, Hazelnut & 146
Chocolate Mousse 170
Coconut Puddings 80
Coleslaw with Sumac & Pastrami 95
Corn Chowder, Leek & 44
courgette see zucchini
Couscous Salad, Pearl 154
Crème Patissèrie 158
Cucumber Pickle Salad 21
Cucumber Slices, Sweet & Sour 164
Cucumber Tzatziki 151

desserts
    Blueberry Sour Cream Cake 38
    Chocolate Mousse 170
    Crème Patissèrie 158
    Hazelnut Meringue Layers 170
    Lime, Hazelnut & Chocolate Cream Pie 146
    Orange & Almond Syrup Cake 96
    Panforte 172
    Peach & Lemon Semifreddo 23
    Peaches stuffed with Amaretti Biscuits 23
    Pear & Ginger Upside-down Cake 106
    Pear & Hazelnut Crumble Cake 52
    Persimmon Cakes with Passionfruit Icing 67
    Rhubarb & Walnut Cake 133
    Steamed Coconut Puddings 80
    Strawberry Flan 158
Diced Tomato Guacamole 62
Dry-Roasted Potatoes 141

eggplant see aubergine

Fig & Bacon Crumble 166
fish and seafood
    Baked Seafood & Nori Rolls 124
    Fresh Tuna with Avocado 62
    Prawn Cocktail 164
    Seafood Filo Pies 58
    Smoked Fish Roulade 31
    Spicy Salmon Cakes 15
    Sumac-Crusted Salmon 152
    Tunisian Fish Tajine 91
Flan, Strawberry with Crème Patissèrie 158
Focaccia Bread 157
Fresh Tuna with Avocado 62
fritters see also panelle
Fritters, Spinach & Feta 87
Fruit Mince 170

Ginger, Pear &, Upside-down Cake 106
Green Beans, Caramelised Pumpkin & Roasted Walnut Salad 50
Green Garden Soup 28
Green Olive Pesto 113
Grilled Polenta 118
Grilled Tomatoes with Braised Red Onion 64
Guacamole, Diced Tomato 62

Hazelnut Meringue Layers 170
Hazelnut Salsa, Avocado & 124
Horseradish Rouille 152
Hummus 154

Kaffir Lime & Palm Sugar Syrup 80
kumara see sweet potato

lamb
    Butterflied Leg of 48
    Lamb Skewers with Lemon Grass & Ginger 20
    Lamb Souvlaki 151
Leek & Corn Chowder 44
Lemon & Almond Biscuits 121
Lemon & Caper Sauce 31

Lemon, Caper & Celery Stuffing 126
Lime, Hazelnut & Chocolate Cream Pie 146

Mango Salsa 164
Meatballs, Sicilian 117
Meringue Layers 170
Middle Eastern Salads 93, 94, 95
Moroccan Honeyed Tomato Salad 94
Mushroom-Filled Pancakes 131
Mushroom Ragù, Shinbeef, Bacon & 101
Mushroom Salad, Warm 142

Nori Rolls 124

Olive Pesto, Green 113
Olives (Black), Potatoes with Rosemary, Cherry Tomatoes & 47
Olives, Grilled Polenta topped with Mushrooms 118
Onions, Caramelised 141
Orange & Almond Biscuits 122
Orange & Almond Syrup Cake 96
Orange & Fennel Marinade 48
Orzo Salad, Spinach 151

Pancakes, Mushroom-Filled 131
Pancakes, Zucchini & Noodle 78
Panelle (Fritters), Chickpea 113
Panforte 172
Parsnip, Leek & Parmesan Terrine 103
Passionfruit Icing 67
Pastrami, Coleslaw with Sumac & 95
pastry and pies
   Asparagus & Rice Tart 138
   Lime, Hazelnut & Chocolate Cream Pie 146
   Seafood Filo Pies 58
   Silverbeet, Apple & Parmesan Pie 59
   Spicy Diced Pork in Wonton Cones 74
   Strawberry Flan with Crème Patissèrie 158
   Sweet Potato & Sage Ricotta Tart 65
Peach & Lemon Semifreddo 23
Peach, Grapefruit & Pear Salad 18

Peaches stuffed with Amaretti Biscuits 23
Pear & Ginger Upside-down Cake 106
Pear & Hazelnut Crumble Cake 52
Pearl Couscous Salad 154
Persimmon Cakes with Passionfruit Icing 67
Pesto, Green Olive 113
Pesto, Basil 154
Plum Paste 53
Plum Sauce, Sweet 32
Polenta, Grilled topped with Mushrooms & Olives 118
Porcini Mushrooms, Artichoke, Parsnip & Apple Soup with 99
pork
   Pork & Lemon with Sweet Chilli Sauce 16
   Pork Chops baked with Apples, Fennel & Grapes 120
   Pork Fillet stuffed with Spinach & Plums 32
   Sicilian Meatballs 117
   Slow-Baked Pork Belly Slices 76
   Spicy Diced Pork in Wonton Cones 74
potatoes
   Dry-Roasted Potatoes 141
   Potatoes with Rosemary, Cherry Tomatoes & Black Olives 47
   Roasted Potatoes with a Spicy Tomato Sauce 127
   Sage Roasted Potatoes 168
   Sweet Potato & Sage Ricotta Tart 65
Prawn Cocktail 164
preserves
   Fruit Mince 170
   Plum Paste 53
   Plum Sauce, Sweet 32
   Preserved Lemon 89
   Red Capsicum & Mustardseed Marmalade 48
Pumpkin, Roasted with Cashew Nuts & Sesame Dressing 104

Red Capsicum & Mustardseed Marmalade 48
Redcurrant Sauce 126

Rhubarb & Walnut Cake 133
rice
   Arancine – Rice Balls with Beef Ragù 114
   Asparagus & Rice Tart 138
   Baked Seafood & Nori Rolls 124
   Risotto Pancakes with Tomato & Grilled Capsicum 45
Roasted Beetroot with Red Onions & Chorizo 36
Roasted Cauliflower & Asian Greens 79
Roasted Potatoes, Sage 168
Roasted Potatoes with a Spicy Tomato Sauce 127
Roasted Pumpkin with Cashew Nuts & Sesame Dressing 104
Roasted Vegetable Parcels 169
Roasted Vegetable Sauce 118
Roasted Vegetable Salad with Sumac-Crusted Salmon 152

Sage Roasted Potatoes 168
salads
   Asparagus Salad 145
   Carrot & Harissa Salad 93
   Coleslaw with Sumac & Pastrami 95
   Cucumber Pickle Salad 21
   Diced Tomato Guacamole 62
   Green Beans, Caramelised Pumpkin & Roasted Walnut Salad 50
   Middle Eastern Salads 93, 94, 95
   Moroccan Honeyed Tomato Salad 94
   Peach, Grapefruit & Pear Salad 18
   Pearl Couscous Salad 154
   Prawn Cocktail 164
   Roasted Beetroot with Red Onions & Chorizo 36
   Roasted Vegetable Salad 152
   Smoked Chicken Salad with Sundried Tomatoes, Olives & Feta 149
   Soba Noodle Salad 73
   Spinach Orzo Salad 151
   Sweet & Sour Cucumber Slices 164

Vegetable Salad, Roasted 52
Warm Mushroom Salad 142
Warm Spinach Salad 128
Salmon Cakes, Spicy 15
Salmon, Sumac-Crusted 152
Salsa, Mango 164
Salt-Baked Chicken 139

sauces
- Aubergine & Tomato Sauce 60
- Capsicum Sauce 58
- Horseradish Rouille 152
- Lemon & Caper Sauce 31
- Plum Sauce, Sweet 32
- Red Capsicum & Mustardseed Marmalade 49
- Redcurrant Sauce 126
- Roasted Vegetable Sauce 118
- Spinach Sauce 131
- Sweet Chilli Sauce 16
- Sweet Plum Sauce 33
- Walnut, Capsicum & Cumin Sauce 139

Seafood Filo Pies 58
Sesame Dressing 104
Shinbeef, Bacon & Mushroom Ragù 101
Sicilian Meatballs 117
Silverbeet, Apple & Parmesan Pie 59
Slow-Baked Pork Belly Slices 76
Smoked Beef, Asparagus Salad 145
Smoked Chicken Salad with Sundried Tomatoes 149
Smoked Fish Roulade 31

Soba Noodle Salad 73

soups
- Artichoke, Parsnip & Apple Soup 99
- Green Garden Soup 28
- Leek & Corn Chowder 44
- Spicy Zucchini Soup 73

Souvlaki, Lamb 151
Spinach & Feta Fritters 87
Spinach Orzo Salad 151
Spinach Salad, Warm 128
Spinach Sauce 131
Steamed Coconut Puddings 80
Strawberry Flan with Crème Patissèrie 158
Sumac-Crusted Salmon 152
Sweet & Sour Cucumber Slices 164
Sweet Balsamic Syrup 131
Sweet Potato & Sage Ricotta Tart 65

Tajine of Lamb Shanks 89
Tajine, Tunisian Fish 91
Terrine, Parsnip, Leek & Parmesan 103
Tomato Salad, Moroccan Honeyed 94
Tomato Sauce, Spicy 127
Tomatoes, Grilled with Braised Red Onion 64
Tuna, Fresh with Avocado & Diced Tomato Guacamole 62
Tunisian Fish Tajine 91
Turkey, Butterflied 166
Tzatziki, Cucumber 151

Veal Schnitzel Rolls 126

vegetable dishes
- Asparagus & Rice Tart 138
- Aubergine, Tomato & Gruyère Torte 35
- Caramelised Onions 141
- Chickpea Panelle (Fritters) 113
- Dry-Roasted Potatoes topped with Caramelised Onions 141
- Green Beans, Caramelised Pumpkin & Roasted Walnut Salad 50
- Grilled Polenta topped with Mushrooms & Olives 118
- Grilled Tomatoes with Braised Red Onion 64
- Mushroom-Filled Pancakes 131
- Parsnip, Leek & Parmesan Terrine 103
- Pearl Couscous Salad 154
- Potatoes with Rosemary, Cherry Tomatoes & Black Olives 47
- Risotto Pancakes with Tomato & Grilled Capsicum 45
- Roasted Cauliflower & Asian Greens 79
- Roasted Potatoes with a Spicy Tomato Sauce 127
- Roasted Pumpkin with Cashew Nuts 104
- Roasted Vegetable Parcels 169
- Roasted Vegetable Salad 152
- Sage Roasted Potatoes 168
- Silverbeet, Apple & Parmesan Pie 59
- Soba Noodle Salad 73
- Spicy Roasted Yams with Sumac 105
- Spinach & Feta Fritters 87
- Spinach Orzo Salad 151
- Sweet Potato & Sage Ricotta Tart 65
- Zucchini & Noodle Pancakes 78

Venison Slices 154

Walnut Biscuits, Cheese & 100
Walnut Cake, Rhubarb & 133
Warm Mushroom Salad 142
Warm Spicy Dressing 79
Warm Spinach Salad 128
Wonton Cones, Spicy Diced Pork in 75

Yams, Spicy Roasted with Sumac 105

Zucchini & Noodle Pancakes 78
Zucchini Soup 73